Praise for *Jesus the Refugee*

"How would Jesus and his family fare as refugees if they fled from Herod today? The answer: not well at all. This hypothetical case allows Butner to educate us on the complexities and injustices of the current international refugee and asylum system. This is a thorough, provocative study grounded in our faith and attuned to the crises of global migration."
—M. Daniel Carroll R. (Rodas), PhD, Scripture Press Ministries Professor of Biblical Studies and Pedagogy, Wheaton College and Graduate School

"Christian ethics has a long tradition of looking to find the face of Christ in the faces of the most vulnerable. This deeply researched book accomplishes this with great sophistication and theological acuity, while challenging common misconceptions surrounding refugees. Those who read it will find their understanding of the topic enhanced and their compassion stimulated."
—Fellipe do Vale, PhD, assistant professor of biblical and systematic theology, Trinity Evangelical Divinity School

"Too many accounts of migration ethics depend on affections or good wishes, but in centering his account of refugees through the story of the holy family, Glenn Butner offers us a refreshing, scripturally grounded, and politically informed account of refugee solidarity. For Butner, to care for refugees is to care for those bearing the image of Christ's own family. A crisp and accessible work for those looking to bring together Scripture and an ethic of migration."
—Myles Werntz, associate professor of theology, director of Baptist studies, Abilene Christian University

"Butner's innovative idea to examine whether Jesus and his family would have been granted asylum today is a must-read for those who want to turn their compassion into concrete acts of solidarity on behalf of refugees. This well-researched book demonstrates clearly and compellingly that in this world, where the right to asylum is increasingly restricted, it is simply not enough to be deserving of protection in order to receive it. Thank you for writing it."

—Danielle Vella, author of *Dying to Live: Stories from Refugees on the Road to Freedom* and director, Global Reconciliation Program, Jesuit Refugee Service

"Don't miss Glenn Butner's book, *Jesus the Refugee*. It will startle Christians who root for the holy family fleeing to Egypt, but are fearful of or indifferent to today's migrants. Using his considerable skills as a theologian, ethicist, and economist, Butner ably breaks down today's devilishly complex legal regime and then shows how the holy family would not likely have found safety from Herod if today's refugee laws had applied and how Christians today are called to solidarity with refugees because Jesus aligned himself with refugees. In focusing on how modern law would have treated Jesus, Butner also brings to life the dilemmas faced by today's migrants and the push-and-pull factors that drive their desperate journeys. He explains how the holy family likely faced the same obstacles and made similar choices that today would see them branded law-breakers, thieves, and someone else's problem. Butner's work presents fresh and compelling insights into our Christian obligation to all people fleeing danger."

—Linda Dakin-Grimm, lawyer and author of *Dignity and Justice: Welcoming the Stranger at Our Border*

JESUS THE REFUGEE

JESUS THE REFUGEE

Ancient Injustice and Modern Solidarity

D. Glenn Butner Jr.

Fortress Press
Minneapolis

JESUS THE REFUGEE
Ancient Injustice and Modern Solidarity

Cover design: Kristin Miller
Cover image: *The Exiles* by Lou Davis

Print ISBN: 978-1-5064-7936-1
eBook ISBN: 978-1-5064-7938-5

To the members of Sterling College's working
group on Latino/a Hospitality:

Maritza Chavez, Nicole Marin, Estephany Moncada,
Miguel Salmeron, Gonzalo Serrano, and Mark Tremaine

Contents

Acknowledgments

I HAVE MANY PEOPLE TO thank for the development of this book. *Jesus the Refugee* would not exist without my friend and Fortress editor Ryan Hemmer, who encouraged me to write a book proposal when I asked him if there was anything to this idea. Thanks also to the anonymous reviewers at *Political Theology* who had previously rejected an article by the same name—this project truly needed to be a book, not an academic article. Myles Werntz and Linda Dakin-Grimm provided helpful reading suggestions as the project was just beginning. Roy Millhouse and Tim Gabrielson provided tremendous support in understanding the first-century context throughout the writing of the book. I am thankful for such good friends and department members. Initial work on the concept was enhanced through a grant from the Council for Christian Colleges & Universities obtained by

Paul Brandes, which resulted in a fruitful virtual discussion with Tisha Rajendra, one of my favorite immigration ethicists. My sister Jessie Butner joined me for a virtual book club on refugees during the pandemic, helping me attempt to articulate my ideas clearly. Sia Joung, Kappa Kaoma, Estephany Moncada, and Emile Ngiruwonsanga Nigiriyo kindly shared their immigration experiences to help open my eyes to some possible experiences of immigrants. During the production of the book, Laurel Watney and Mikki Millhouse helped bring in hundreds of items via interlibrary loan. They remain the invisible force behind much of my writing. Christian Dashiell, Karen Keen, Amber Diaz Pearson, and Myles Werntz all agreed to do a complete read-through of the work to provide feedback. I completely rewrote several sections and the final two chapters with their feedback in mind, resulting in a much stronger book. Linda Dakin-Grimm caught two mistakes in my explanation of legal matters while reading the book as an endorser, helping me reduce factual errors in my account. Elvis Ramirez and Brianna Blackburn at Scribe Inc. did an excellent job in copyediting, especially in cleaning up the bibliography I submitted, which was in a worse state than it should have been. As always, my wife, Lydia, was supportive and encouraging throughout this project, especially helping me stay focused on God's grace and justice while reading about such unjust circumstances.

I want to especially acknowledge those who have played a role in my ongoing awakening to the experiences of refugees and other immigrants and to the need for substantial change in the international refuge regime. Thanks to the community and churches in La Carpio, Costa Rica; to the employees at B&M Storage and Distribution formerly in Winston-Salem, North Carolina; to those associated with Lutheran Family Services in

Chapel Hill, North Carolina; to the staff and inmates at the Federal Corrections Complex in Butner, North Carolina; to the students and volunteers at the International Language Center in Milwaukee, Wisconsin; and most recently, to the Latina/o Hospitality Working Group at Sterling College in Sterling, Kansas. I dedicate this work to the students, faculty, and staff of this final group who worked so diligently to improve Sterling College's institutional solidarity with immigrants.

1

Jesus the Refugee?

I WAS WALKING DOWN A dusty road in La Carpio, Costa Rica, my hands working to make a flower out of colored pieces of pipe cleaner to place into the hands of a young girl at the front of a growing line of children who were following me and my friends as we slowly walked our way out of the community. I knew that many of the residents of La Carpio were Nicaraguan refugees, but at eighteen years old, I had little sense of what this meant or why most residents lived in small shacks made of corrugated steel with no running water and few economic prospects. I had come with the senior class at my Christian high school to lead Bible camps and work on small construction projects as part of a short-term mission trip. Before a Bible camp started, I had made a pipe cleaner flower on a whim for a child waiting for the event, and the small trinket was such a hit that nearly an hour later, several friends and I, faced with a crowd of excited potential owners, were still making the flowers, working through the last of the pipe cleaners on our walk back to the bus, happy to provide the children with something that would brighten their day.

Despite seeing their struggles firsthand, and despite going on to take extensive coursework in political science and economics as an undergraduate student, I did not begin to understand the international political, legal, and economic forces that left so many trapped in a slum like La Carpio. I was moved to compassion, but I did not grasp the reasons why these Nicaraguans were in a situation that prompted my compassion. I had no genuine understanding. Only years later did I learn that, though hundreds of thousands had fled to Costa Rica from unstable and war-torn neighboring countries in the 1980s and early '90s, only fifty thousand had received official refugee status, and this status was the key to having any legal claim to protection, work, or political participation.[1] Without official refugee status, an estimated 260,000 Nicaraguan undocumented immigrants fleeing conflict would not even have guaranteed access to humanitarian aid.[2] I had thought a refugee was merely someone who had fled conflict, and I had no idea of the more technical legal definition or of the protections that were limited to those who met the technical definition through a complex legal process. I certainly did not know that Costa Rican perceptions of Nicaraguan migrants as prone to crime and disease had led to resistance against their acceptance[3] or that Costa Rican law put a cap on the percentage

---

1 James Wiley, "Undocumented Aliens and Recognized Refugees: The Right to Work in Costa Rica," *International Migration Review* 29, no. 2 (Summer 1995): 423.

2 This estimate is based on Costa Rican governmental claims. The United Nations High Commissioner for Refugees (UNHCR) places the number considerably lower. María Christina García, *Seeking Refuge: Central American Migration to Mexico, the United States, and Canada* (Berkeley: University of California Press, 2006), 39.

3 Wiley, "Undocumented Aliens," 426.

of immigrant workers a firm could hire (until the law was struck down by the Costa Rican Supreme Court after a full decade of refugees entering the country).[4] Such laws meant that even legally recognized refugees would have difficulty obtaining work, keeping many trapped in poverty. Moreover, those who did find work often had to leave their families behind in camps or urban slums where there were no jobs, and once employed, their families no longer qualified for any government assistance.[5] All of these factors made it quite difficult to escape extreme poverty. At the time, I was content to feel compassion and to act in small ways, whether through a minor construction project or my pipe cleaner flowers. Such acts were well intended but cannot begin to address the deeper flaws in the international refugee system. I suspect many Christians find themselves in a similar situation: moved to compassion, perhaps briefly exposed to refugees, but generally uneducated about the global refugee system.

From time to time, I reflect on my naivete in La Carpio and wonder what that experience can teach me about my faith. I now realize there is another refugee story that I approached with equal naivete: the refugee flight of Jesus, Mary, and Joseph as described in Matthew 2:13–15, following the visit of the magi who had inadvertently informed Herod of the birth of a baby who was a potential rival to the throne: "When [the magi] had departed, behold, an angel of the Lord appeared to Joseph in a dream and said, 'Rise, take the child and his mother, flee to Egypt, and stay there until I tell you. Herod is going to search for the child to

---

4 Wiley, 429–33. By law, 90 percent of employees had to be Costa Rican citizens, and 85 percent of all payroll expenses had to go to citizens. Exceptions were made for small firms with five or fewer employees. The law was struck down in 1990 for violating the terms of the 1951 UN Refugee Protocol, which Costa Rica had signed and which will be discussed in chapter 2 of this book.

5 Gilda Pacheco, *Nicaraguan Refugees in Costa Rica: Adjustment to Camp Life* (Washington, DC: Center for Immigration Policy and Refugee Assistance, 1989), 17–18.

destroy him.' Joseph rose and took the child and his mother by night and departed for Egypt. He stayed there until the death of Herod, that what the Lord had said through the prophet might be fulfilled, 'Out of Egypt I called my Son'" (NASB). From an early point in my faith, this passage challenged me to care for refugees. After all, if my own Savior and Lord was a refugee, then surely I should care for those who face the same dangers he did. The holy family's flight to Egypt has provided an impulse toward solidarity with refugees among a wide range of Christian commentators, from evangelical Bible scholars to liberationist ethicists to Roman Catholic popes.[6] Understanding Jesus as a refugee is a well-established idea in the Christian tradition. For example, during the sixteenth-century Reformations, Martin Luther preached on Matthew 2:13–23, drawing on the idea of Jesus as a refugee to teach Protestants fearful of invading Catholic armies that Jesus is our example in fleeing for safety: "If we can flee for refuge, we ought not despise this expedient, as certain enthusiasts do."[7] During World War I, the Russian journal *Rodina* depicted a refugee family next to the holy family in a drawing called "Two Flights," seeking to develop concern for refugees among its readership.[8] Examples could be multiplied. There is a broad and deep consensus that Jesus was a refugee and that this matters for Christian ethics. The problem is that such claims often naively ignore the fact that it is quite unlikely that the holy family would have

---

6 For example, see James K. Hoffmeier, *The Immigration Crisis: Immigrants, Aliens, and the Bible* (Wheaton, IL: Crossway, 2009), 131–35; Miguel A. De La Torre, *The U.S. Immigration Crisis: Toward an Ethics of Place* (Eugene, OR: Cascade, 2016), 114, 154–55; and Pius XII, *Exsul Familia Nazarethana* (1952), accessed December 12, 2021, https://www.papalencyclicals.net/pius12/p12exsul.htm.

7 Martin Luther, "The Day of the Holy Innocents," in *The Complete Sermons of Martin Luther*, vol. 7, ed. Eugene F. A. Klug, trans. Eugene F. A. Klug et al. (Grand Rapids, MI: Baker, 2000), §21, §16.

8 Peter Gatrell, *The Making of the Modern Refugee* (Oxford: Oxford University Press, 2013), 35–36.

refugee status under our current international refugee regime, and this lack of status should be central to any Christian ethical analysis of the modern refugee system.[9]

In common usage, the word *refugee* is taken to refer to anyone fleeing danger, but in law, to be a refugee is to possess a status that guarantees certain rights, protections, and opportunities. The political and legal dimensions of the term are essential to its practical meaning, but few seem to grasp the complexity of that title or its application to Jesus, Mary, and Joseph. As Emma Haddad explains, the terminology of being a refugee is complexified by several facts. First, the term *refugee* includes a value judgment concerning who is deserving of protection—refugees are protected and provided for by various international, governmental, nonprofit institutions where other migrants may not be. Second, the term *refugee* is constrained by political agendas that may seek to expand or restrict benefits and rights associated with the status in order to increase or restrict immigration. Third, there are various layers of political institutions within which the term is applied, and each political institution may have a different definition of what counts as a refugee.[10] In other words, if we are considering whether Jesus counts as a refugee, we must ask, "to whom?" Certainly, many Christians from a wide range of theological, ethical, and political convictions consider Jesus

---

9 This is contrary to the position of Markus Zehnder, who argues that "there is no doubt that Jesus—together with his parents—would qualify as 'refugee(s)' in the context of current legal standards" (73). Zehnder goes on to insist that Matthew 2 has "no bearing on issues of migration beyond instances of personal persecution or death threats" and that the story is "not related to . . . situations in which large-scale immigration takes place" (75). I consider this conclusion to be rooted in a broad neglect of the realities of migration by displaced persons today combined with a deficient view of the biblical ethic of migration. Zehnder's broader work will be addressed in footnotes at several key points throughout this work. See Markus Zehnder, *The Bible and Immigration: A Critical and Empirical Reassessment* (Eugene, OR: Pickwick, 2021), 73–75.

10 Emma Haddad, *The Refugee in International Society: Between Sovereigns* (Cambridge: Cambridge University Press, 2008), 25–27.

a refugee, but their judgment has no legal significance. Yet it is the legal question that is most pressing for refugees today who are seeking the protection, provision, and inclusion the law provides. In other words, the common theological instinct to describe Jesus as a refugee masks a deeper question: Would Jesus receive refugee status today? This book is an attempt to answer this deeper question.

Of course, the holy family's flight to Egypt occurred thousands of years ago under a different political system and with different economic, legal, cultural, and social realities, so the question of whether Jesus would count as a refugee in our modern refugee system is a theoretical question. But it is important, nonetheless. Its answer is deeply practical, for the hypothetical fate of the holy family in the modern refugee system mirrors the fate of countless families seeking recognition as refugees today. To ask whether Jesus would receive refugee status in our modern system is to move beyond pleas for compassion toward an inquiry into the legal, political, historical, and economic realities that the term *refugee* denotes. My hope is that this inquiry will ultimately compel a response of solidarity.

I intend to pursue a thought experiment requiring three suppositions. First, this book will imagine that modern refugee law (beginning with the 1951 United Nations Convention Relating to the Status of Refugees) was in effect during the holy family's first-century flight to Egypt. This supposition will make it possible to apply modern legal definitions to the circumstances of Matthew 2. Second, this book will analyze the flight while treating Egypt and Judaea according to the geopolitical realities of the first century. In other words, I will continue to assume that Judaea was governed by Herod the Great, who was himself under the rule of the Roman Empire, which also controlled Egypt. This supposition allows us to analyze the acts of the holy family within the historical circumstances that prompted the flight to Egypt as well as struggle with the factor of the flight occurring entirely within the boundaries of the Roman Empire, something that will complexify and perhaps confound the case for counting Jesus as a refugee. Third, this thought experiment will imagine that in the first century, the United States of America and the European Union (EU) were both geopolitical entities with their current refugee law codes, border security apparatuses, and immigration-regulating institutions in place in a modern, globalized context that would make it possible, for example, for Joseph and Mary to seek asylum in the European Union or attempt to be resettled in the United States from a refugee camp or from a temporary settlement in an urban setting. Paradoxically, this third supposition will require us to imagine the concurrent existence of the Roman Empire and the European Union, whose territories overlapped to a significant degree.[11] This supposition is necessary, however, to fully analyze the legal question, since UN refugee guidelines are always contextualized in particular political contexts and since the European Union and United States are two sought-after destinations for refugees. For this reason, the thought experiment will limit consideration to US and EU refugee laws. The book asks whether Jesus, Mary, and Joseph would receive protection within the United States or European Union, given modern refugee law, if they fled from Judaea to Egypt under the actual historical circumstances of their flight.

---

11 Notably, I will not imagine the concurrent existence of modern Israel and first-century Judaea, as this would further complicate matters given that it might require the involvement of the United Nations Relief and Work Agency for Palestinian Refugees (UNRWA), which operates under distinct institutional and legal parameters in comparison with the United Nations High Commissioner for Refugees (UNHCR).

For simplicity's sake, it was necessary to streamline this thought experiment, especially with respect to domestic law. Each nation-state will incorporate the standards of international law into its own judicial, legal, and political frameworks. Each will also have distinct institutional and political constraints on politically feasible courses of action. For the sake of this thought experiment, I will focus on the broad international standards, referencing the situation of specific nation-states to illustrate how these standards work in practice. Yet I will remain unable to fully chart the immigration policy of all EU member states, for example. Certain other differences between modern refugee situations and the one facing the holy family in antiquity will be addressed in greater detail later, but for the present, I should note that at various stages, I will need to identify areas of similarity and difference between the sociopolitical situation in antiquity and that of the modern world. Border security, for instance, is far more substantial today than in antiquity, as are the complexities of the documents required to legally cross borders, factors that prevent us from too easily correlating the circumstances of Jesus, Mary, and Joseph with those facing the typical modern refugee. Throughout this work, my goal will be to establish an adequate comparison for an accurate assessment of the broad contours of the modern international refugee regime, recognizing that each issue could be discussed with much greater technical detail.

Within the parameters of this thought experiment, it will become clear that it is possible to call Jesus a refugee, though this legal status remains a fragile and uncertain possibility. The act of demonstrating that the holy family possessed this status with all associated legal rights would no doubt be contestable in both legal contexts considered; it is in no way guaranteed. Yet it is in the context of the fragility and contestability of designating

Christ as a refugee that we can discover moral and theological significance beyond what is uncovered when we move too quickly to count Jesus as a refugee without considering the legal and political dimensions of that title. Like the Nicaraguan refugees in La Carpio, whose daily lives were shaped by a legal and political system completely unknown to me, we will see that Jesus and his family would face similar challenges today, in all likelihood falling through the cracks of institutional support networks for refugees.

I will proceed in several steps. First, in chapter 2, I will explain the standard legal definition of a refugee and consider what it would take for the holy family to prove to a modern court of law that they possessed this status. Chapter 3 will explore the main reason why Jesus, Mary, and Joseph would likely be disqualified as refugees—they fled to the wrong location. This fact raises the question of why a refugee, or any migrant, chooses a particular destination, a question also explored in this chapter. In chapter 4, I consider what would happen if the holy family chose to relocate to a destination where they could receive refugee status, particularly emphasizing how the European Union and United States would try to prevent this move through the use of force or the denial of a trial in court. Then in chapter 5, I examine typical misconceptions about immigrants that lead the citizens of many nations to resist welcoming refugees. After surveying these various aspects of the holy family's flight, chapter 6 will explore the ethical response Christians are called to make, centering on the principles of solidarity, restitution, and relationship. Chapter 7 will then consider what solidarity looks like in practice, covering its incarnational, institutional, and conflictual dimensions. Only after we have recognized the fragile possibility of Jesus being a refugee and how his story in important respects mirrors the patterns of modern refugees can we consider the necessary ethical and theological implications of using the word *refugee* as a Christological title. My hope is that this thought experiment can move some readers from uninformed compassion to informed action. Before we can reach such conclusions, we must begin with the story of Joseph's dream and his hurried escape from Herod.

2

A Day in Court

"JOSEPH ROSE AND TOOK THE child and his mother by night and departed for Egypt" (Matt 2:14). Like so many refugee stories, this one begins with an unexpected and sudden departure in the middle of the night. An angel had warned Joseph to flee and sent him to Egypt, and he faithfully obeyed, but I imagine many questions swirled through Joseph's mind as he woke his family and prepared them to escape the threat of Herod. What if the Egyptians turned him back? How would he keep his son and wife safe? Once he arrived in Egypt, how would he provide for his family? What sort of hostility or resistance might he find in this strange land? Joseph undoubtedly trusted God with answers to these questions. After all, an angel of the Lord had already appeared to Joseph to announce that the child he was taking to Egypt to protect had been conceived "through the Holy Spirit" and would "save his people from their sins" (Matt 1:20–21). Clearly, this was a child that God wanted to protect, and God certainly had the power to do so, but I suspect that Joseph still wondered how God would get them safely to Egypt. Joseph woke his family, and they fled for Egypt.

In modern international law, families fleeing danger have the greatest hope of finding welcome, avoiding being returned to the homeland they are fleeing, and securing a job and income if they are recognized as refugees. Acquiring this recognition involves a legal process whose details vary by the country in which refuge is sought but whose overarching structure is determined by the 1951 Convention Relating to the Status of Refugees (or the 1951 Refugee Convention for short), a United Nations (UN) treaty that was designed to manage refugees in the aftermath of World War II and remains the centerpiece of international refugee law today. If Jesus, Mary, and Joseph sought refuge today, they would do so according to the dictates of this treaty. In this chapter, I outline the basic components of the 1951 Refugee Convention and describe how the holy family might seek to secure recognition as refugees according to its statutes.

Defining Refugees and Their Rights

According to the 1951 Refugee Convention, a refugee is anyone who, "owing to a well-founded fear of being persecuted for reasons of race, religion, nationality, membership of a particular social group or political opinion, is outside the country of his nationality and is unable, or owing to such fear, is unwilling to avail himself of the protection of that country" (Article

1 A).[1] The term *refugee* typically refers to those who meet this standard and are applying for protection from outside of the territory where refuge is sought, perhaps from a refugee camp or a temporary urban settlement, while the term *asylee* is used for someone who has crossed a border and entered a territory and then sought refuge under the 1951 Refugee Convention, or some other relevant legal standard, within that territory.[2] *Asylee* is a more ambiguous term, since no international legal standard defines asylum.[3] Those who are fleeing danger but do not fit the convention's definition are sometimes called nonconvention refugees. If protected by another law or convention, such nonconvention refugees may also be labeled nonexpellable irregulars. In international law, a person is technically a refugee the moment they meet this standard; courts do not confer refugee status but rather recognize it.[4] The duration of this chapter will unpack the meaning of this definition, but for now, this brief overview will suffice.

Refugees are entitled to a range of rights under the 1951 convention—perhaps most significantly, protection from refoulement, a term referring to the forcible return to the country from which one has fled (Article 33). In addition, refugees are

---

1 The convention also identified as refugees those who were named as such under prior treaties and those without a nationality who had a well-founded fear of persecution in their place of habitual residence. The former case is practically irrelevant seventy years later, while the second is rare and so will not be treated in this work.

2 See the clarifying explanation in David W. Haines, *Immigration Structures and Immigrant Lives: An Introduction to the US Experience* (Lanham, MD: Rowman & Littlefield, 2017), 60–61. Other relevant legal standards will be discussed at other points in this work.

3 Guy S. Goodwin-Gill, "The International Law of Refugee Protection," in *The Oxford Handbook of Refugee and Forced Migration Studies*, ed. Elena Fiddian-Qasmiyeh et al. (Oxford: Oxford University Press, 2014), 42.

4 See discussions in Andreas Zimmermann and Claudia Mahler, "Article 1 A, para. 2," in *The 1951 Convention Relating to the Status of Refugees and Its 1967 Protocol: A Commentary*, ed. Andreas Zimmermann et al. (Oxford: Oxford University Press, 2011), 299; and Guy S. Goodwin-Gill and Jane McAdam, *The Refugee in International Law*, 3rd ed. (Oxford: Oxford University Press, 2007), 51.

guaranteed the right to free movement within the host nation (Article 26), access to public welfare and social security provisions available to natives (Articles 23 and 24), the right to gainful employment (Article 17), access to public education (Article 22), and the right to receive travel documents from the host country if their documentation from their homeland is invalid (Article 27), among other rights. Broadly speaking, whatever rights the refugee's home country was denying are protected and provided by the host country according to the 1951 Refugee Convention. The host nation may provide such rights either as a new permanent home or on a temporary basis until refugees are resettled into another country or repatriated to their home country once it is safe to do so.

The 1951 convention has grown in acceptance and scope. It was originally designed to deal with refugees in Europe at the end of World War II and so had language restricting its applicability to persons in Europe (Introduction B)[5] who were displaced due to events prior to January 1, 1951 (Article 1 A). The convention went into effect shortly after the creation of the United Nations High Commissioner for Refugees (UNHCR) in 1950, which was originally set up as a "nonoperational" body to preserve the national interests of other countries, letting nongovernmental organizations (NGOs) help refugees on the ground.[6] These geographic and temporal restrictions were partly in place to ease signing nations' concerns about the potential costs of a nonoperational body with an open-ended mandate like the UNHCR.[7] Eventually, the geographic restrictions and temporal

---

5 The convention allowed signing countries to decide whether to limit the scope to Europe or to include other regions.
6 Gatrell, *Modern Refugee*, 109.
7 Goodwin-Gill, "International Law," 37.

scope were eliminated through the 1967 Protocol Relating to the Status of Refugees, which otherwise retained the main features of the 1951 convention. While many European nations signed the convention quickly, the United States never did (though its 1968 ratification of the 1967 Protocol means it has still accepted the convention of '51's premises).[8] These premises have been the backbone of recent US law, including the United States Refugee Act of 1980. Today, the 1951 Refugee Convention and/or the 1967 Protocol have been adopted by 145 nation-states.

The Holy Family's Case for Recognition

To determine whether Mary and Joseph are refugees in the imagined scenario of this book, we must consider four points: (1) whether they had a well-founded fear of persecution; (2) whether this fear met the reasons designated in article 1 of the 1951 Refugee Convention; (3) whether they were outside of the country of their nationality; and (4) whether they were unable or unwilling to find protection in their home country for fear of this persecution. If these four criteria are met, the holy family counts as refugees under modern refugee law and are entitled to the protections discussed above. For the duration of this chapter, I will consider criteria 1, 2, and 4 to aid the reader in understanding the typical refugee process and to begin to expose certain limitations and weak points in the current international system. I will wait to address criterion 3 until the

---

8 Susan Kneebone, *Refugees, Asylum Seekers and the Rule of Law: Comparative Perspectives* (Cambridge: Cambridge University Press, 2009), 124. The United States did not ignore the aftermath of World War II but established its own procedure for refugees through the 1952 Immigration and Nationality Act, a qualification well noted in Mark R. Amstutz, *Just Immigration: American Policy in Christian Perspective* (Grand Rapids, MI: William B. Eerdmans, 2017), 18.

next chapter, since it is the most complicated component of this thought experiment.

Jesus, Mary, and Joseph would have three possible paths toward obtaining protection as refugees. First, they might travel to a refugee camp, where the UNHCR could resettle them after a screening process and after finding a host nation willing to accept them. Until resettlement, the holy family would live in the camp and depend on the UN and/or NGOs to meet their basic needs. Second, the holy family might settle temporarily in a neighboring country while seeking resettlement through the UNHCR. Typically, such refugees live in urban areas rather than camps, often finding work without legal permission, living with relatives or generous strangers, or perhaps even suffering homelessness.[9] Third, they might enter another nation and claim asylum. The holy family might enter legally, perhaps with a tourist visa, and then request asylum, but the slow procedure for securing a legal means of entry in most European and North American nations means that an "illegal" border crossing would be required. (Paradoxically, as we will see in chapter 3, "illegal" entry to seek asylum without documentation by the host nation is by design the default course for refugees, an act considered legal by the standards of international law and some countries' immigration laws.) If the holy family was able to arrive without being detained, they could apply for what is called affirmative asylum, but if they were arrested for crossing a border without documentation, they would likely face defensive asylum

---

9 In 2013, there were twice as many Syrian refugees in Turkey living outside of camps as those living within camps. Reports suggest many lived with relatives, squatted in abandoned buildings, or settled in parks. Lacking passports, many were unable to access public services, notably including education. See Osman Bahadir Dinçir et al., *Turkey and Syrian Refugees: The Limits of Hospitality* (Washington, DC: Brookings Institute, 2013), 16–19.

procedures, so called because the asylum proceedings are a defense against removal from a country. In the United States, affirmative asylum is granted more frequently,[10] while defensive asylum is more challenging because it requires a hearing in court where the outcome can be shaped significantly by the personality and politics of the presiding judge. The holy family would be unlikely to navigate this procedure successfully without legal assistance. But once they found legal representation, the quest to establish their refugee standing could begin.

Well-Founded Fear of Persecution

To fall under the 1951 Refugee Convention's protection, refugees or asylees must have a well-founded fear of persecution. Persecution refers to "a sufficiently severe human rights violation and a determination regarding the perpetrator of the violation."[11] The human rights violation must be substantive—like loss of life, freedom, personal integrity, political rights, or due process rights, among other possibilities.[12] To count as persecution, the perpetrator of the event generally must be the state, though in situations where the state cannot or will not provide protection, persecution may still be occurring.[13] The word *persecution* in the phrase "well-founded fear of persecution" is relatively easy to understand, but "well-founded fear" is a far more complicated matter.

What counts as a well-founded fear of persecution? The idea of fear might be interpreted subjectively, referring to the mental states of a refugee, or objectively, referring to an estimate of the

---

10 Thirty percent of defensive asylum and 74 percent of affirmative asylum petitions were granted in the United States in 2013. Amstutz, *Just Immigration*, 30.
11 Zimmermann and Mahler, "Article 1 A," 345.
12 Zimmermann and Mahler, 355–57.
13 Goodwin-Gill, "International Law," 39.

probability of persecution, or a combination of the two.[14] The objective approach presents many challenges and requires predictions of human behavior that may not be feasible.[15] The drafters of the 1951 Refugee Convention wrote an explanatory note that included past victimization or persecution as a component of objective proof—if one has already been persecuted, it should be reasonably easy to prove a well-founded fear of persecution.[16] Since Herod had not yet directly persecuted the holy family, this approach to an objective claim would not suffice. Instead, a predictive approach would be needed, which would attempt to show the likelihood of persecution if Jesus, Mary, and Joseph remained within Herod's territory. A subjective argument is also unlikely to succeed. In theory, the subjective component must consider the psychology of the individual—that is, how seriously do they hold to the persecuted religious identity? In reality, cultural, psychological, and biological differences make this determination nearly impossible.[17] Undoubtedly, a lawyer representing the holy family in our thought experiment would seek to make an objective claim based on the likelihood of *future* persecution.

Herod was a dangerous leader prone to persecuting his political enemies. First-century Judea was characterized by underlying political resentment that would boil over into revolt whenever there was a power vacuum or when the offense was so strong that even lacking chances of success, the populace was too outraged for restraint.[18] The frequency of such uprisings undoubtedly provided an occasion for Herod to use violence as he sought

14 Niraj Nathwani, *Rethinking Refugee Law: Refugees and Human Rights* (New York: Martinus Nijhoff, 2003), 68.
15 Nathwani, 72.
16 Zimmermann and Mahler, "Article 1 A," 336.
17 Zimmermann and Mahler, 339.
18 N. T. Wright, *The New Testament and the People of God* (Minneapolis: Fortress, 1992), 170–73.

to maintain power. Herod also faced lingering resistance from the Hasmonean dynasty he had replaced (and into whose family he had married). This resulted in growing paranoia, to the extent that he had his own wife Mariamne and two sons tried and executed (at different times) for treason. Later, Antipater, his son by a different wife, met the same fate.[19] First-century historians like Josephus were well aware of Herod's violent tendencies. Josephus shares numerous accounts of Herod resorting to the use of torture and spies.[20] Herod was also known to sell Judeans into slavery.[21] On Josephus's telling, Herod had such a great fear of "discontents" that he prohibited public meetings and even the right to walk together in public.[22] Prohibiting assembly and free movement and taking life without just cause would be significant human rights violations of the sort required to establish objective persecution.

Unfortunately for the holy family, leaving a nation where human rights violations regularly occur is not sufficient to establish a well-founded fear of persecution. The point was made succinctly during the 1980s by a representative of the United States Department of State in a letter to the *New York Times*: "It is not enough for the applicant to state that he faces the same conditions that every other citizen faces. [Under the terms of the 1980 Refugee Act we ask,] Why are you different from everyone else in your country? How have you been singled out, threatened, imprisoned, tortured, harassed?"[23] Without the threat becoming *personal*, it is far less likely that refugee status will be recognized or asylum granted.

---

19 Ben Witherington III, *New Testament History: A Narrative Account* (Grand Rapids, MI: Baker Academic, 2001), 58–60.

20 Josephus, *Antiquities of the Jews*, trans. William Whiston (New York: Lovell & Coryell, n.d., ca. 1900s), 15.7.4; 15.8.4.

21 Josephus, 16.1.1.

22 Josephus, 15.10.5.

23 Quoted in García, *Seeking Refuge*, 89.

It was by such logic that countless Salvadorians and Guatemalans were denied asylum in the 1980s and '90s. In this case, Joseph and Mary could try to appeal to the fact that Magi had told Herod of the birth of a king in Bethlehem (Matt 2:2–6)—surely this would prompt persecution from a ruler such as Herod, who had no intention of yielding his throne. Add to this the fact that Mary and Joseph believed their child to be the Messiah, a title filled with religious and political significance (as we shall see), and a case for establishing well-founded fear begins to come together. Of course, the problem will be establishing these points in a court of law.

The Reason for Persecution

The 1951 Refugee Convention restricts refugee status to those facing persecution, and it strictly identifies the kinds of persecution that are adequate grounds for refugee status: persecution "for reasons of race, religion, nationality, membership of a particular social group or political opinion" is necessary for refugee status (Article 1 A). This definition was crafted in the aftermath of World War II with the specific needs of Europeans in mind. Two factors were important. First, many were fleeing persecution on the basis of social group or political opinion in Soviet-occupied territories, leading refugee law to a focus on such categories. Second, feelings of guilt due to the widespread unwillingness of most nations to welcome Jewish refugees during the Holocaust combined with the desire of many persecuted Jews to relocate, leading to a legal emphasis on such categories as race and religion.[24] European

---

24 Emma Haddad outlines how many refugees from World War II simply refused to be repatriated to their now Soviet-controlled nations while new refugees from Eastern Europe increased. Haddad, *Refugee in International Society*, 130–32. For a concise treatment of the American perspective on Jewish refugees, see Haines, *Immigration Structures*, 34–35.

nations desired to provide protection to such individuals. On the other hand, widespread devastation and displacement due to war and resulting economic chaos could perhaps explain the exclusion of those displaced for economic or military reasons in the refugee status. Those who flee under such conditions cannot qualify as refugees under the UN definition, though they might find protection for other reasons under other legal provisions.

The holy family would meet the criterion of being persecuted as members of a legally relevant category. Jesus would fit the category of "membership in a specific group"—children two and under, a group Herod had targeted for murder (Matt 2:16). A case could also be made for persecution on the basis of political opinion or religion. The magi had viewed Jesus as king of the Jews (Matt 2:2), which would be the political reason for Herod's persecution. We are told in Luke's Gospel that an angel had informed Mary that Jesus would receive "the throne of his father David" (Luke 1:32). Luke is also clear that Mary accepted what she was told (Luke 1:38), meaning that she held the political opinion or religious belief (the two were not sharply distinguished in antiquity), which would be the basis of persecution, though technically a political opinion wrongly attributed by the state to a refugee (who did not hold that opinion) is still sufficient grounds for protection.[25] Jesus, Mary, and Joseph certainly meet this component of the definition. Others seeking safety are not so fortunate.

Many nonconvention refugees face a legitimate need for protection but do not find it under the 1951 Refugee Convention. Those displaced by warfare, for example, are not entitled to protection under the convention. Similarly, the wording of

---

25 Goodwin-Gill and McAdam, *Refugee in International Law*, 87.

the convention tends to envision persecution at the hands of the state, but many nonconvention refugees are fleeing failed states and so cannot meet the necessary criteria to qualify for protection under the 1951 Refugee Convention.[26] European nations tend to offer alternative shorter humanitarian status to those who do not fit the 1951 convention definitions, though specific policies have varied over time. In the 1990s, for example, these alternative protective statuses could range from a waiver of deportation (Germany); to temporary, renewable, one-year humanitarian status with the opportunity to apply for permanent residence after five years (Ireland); to temporary status with a maximum limit of two years (Sweden).[27] Such alternative statuses may include far fewer rights and opportunities—those without documentation but who have a waiver of deportation, for example, would still struggle to find work. In the United States, those who do not meet the technical definition are often incarcerated or expelled unless public pressure leads a president to provide Temporary Protected Status (TPS) to a group of nonconvention refugees. Unfortunately, the presence of public pressure often depends on how many members of a particular ethnic group, nationality, or religious group are already present in the United States. Under-represented groups like Iraqi Kurds might find it particularly difficult to obtain TPS.[28]

Among the gaps in the convention's definition is a lack of protection for women fleeing violence. Persecution on the basis

---

26 Serena Parekh, *No Refuge: Ethics and the Global Refugee Crisis* (Oxford: Oxford University Press, 2020), 33.

27 Karen Duke, Rosemary Sales, and Jeanne Gregory, "Refugee Resettlement in Europe," in *Refugees, Citizenship, and Social Policy in Europe*, ed. Alice Bloch and Carl Levy (London: Macmillan, 1999), 114–16.

28 The role of existing populations in securing TPS or other nonconvention provisions as well as the eccentricities of US refugee policy is a central theme of María Christina García, *The Refugee Challenge in Post–Cold War America* (Oxford: Oxford University Press, 2017).

of gender is not explicitly included under the 1951 Refugee Convention, though there is an international legal precedent to consider some women who are subjected to violence persecuted under the category of "social group." Guy Goodwin-Gil and Jane McAdam explain that when gender-related violence has "political purposes, including the enforcement of conformity to a particular religious, cultural, or social view of society," it may count as persecution. Here, the authors provide the example of French case law, which has allowed that refusal to accept arranged marriages in certain Muslim regions may result in state-sanctioned violence for refusing to conform to this religious and social expectation.[29] Fleeing genital mutilation may also qualify as fleeing persecution in some countries, including the United States.[30] Generally, though, women seeking safety from gender-based violence are not subject to the convention's protection.

A few examples of the situation may illustrate the problem more powerfully. Consider the story of an eleven-year-old Somali girl who fled with her mother to Kampala, Uganda, partly to avoid genital mutilation in her home country. Sometime after her arrival in an unfamiliar land, the girl's mother died. Becoming aware of her situation, the UNHCR sought to refoul her to Somalia, where she would face a heightened risk of gendered violence and genital mutilation as an unaccompanied minor female. It is difficult to imagine the psychological burden her imminent return to danger might have brought. The girl's only known relative lived in the Netherlands, where she could find both family and protection, if the UNHCR sought resettlement and family reunification. Fortunately, in this case, a legal

29 Goodwin-Gill and McAdam, *Refugee in International Law*, 82.
30 Elena Fiddian-Qasmiyeh, "Gender and Forced Migration," in Fiddian-Qasmiyeh et al., *Oxford Handbook*, 399.

advocacy group was able to intervene and find a temporary legal guardian for the girl while seeking efforts to reunite her with her uncle.[31] Many other girls whose stories we will never know have simply been refouled (returned to one's homeland). Elena Fiddian-Qasmiyeh summarizes another much-discussed case: "A man was tied to a chair and forced at gunpoint to watch his common-law wife being raped by soldiers. In determining the case for refugee status, he was deemed to have been tortured. His partner was not."[32] Such stories clearly show unjust and irrational standards that neglect the protection of women under the 1951 Refugee Convention.

Some abused women can find protection after abuse, though this may be less common. For example, sixteen-year-old Liliana fled Honduras after her stepfather threatened her with a machete, the last instance in a long history of abuse. Crossing the US border illegally with the use of a *coyote* (a smuggler to help migrants cross into the United States illegally), Liliana hoped to be reunited with her biological father who was in the United States. She was arrested after entering the country illegally but was soon released from US Customs and Border Protection custody into the care of her father. Unfortunately, her father was also abusive, and the Los Angeles Department of Children and Family Services removed Liliana from her new living situation. With the help of a pro bono lawyer, Liliana was able to secure lawful residence through the Special Immigrant Juvenile Status (SIJS) program.[33] Liliana's protection was contingent on her being a juvenile. Not all persons fleeing

---

31 Guglielmo Verdirame and Barbara Harrell-Bond, *Rights in Exile: Janus-Faced Humanitarianism* (New York: Berghahn, 2005), 123.
32 Fiddian-Qasmiyeh, "Gender and Forced Migration," 398.
33 A fuller version of Liliana's story is available in Linda Dakin-Grimm, *Dignity and Justice: Welcoming the Stranger at Our Border* (Maryknoll, NY: Orbis, 2020), 65–71.

gender-based violence are without protection, but many are, especially during the period when Attorney General Jeff Sessions overturned a rule in 2018 that treated domestic violence as grounds for persecution and refugee status.[34] The ruling was later reestablished in 2021 under Attorney General Merrick Garland.[35]

Those fleeing warfare, natural disaster, gender-based violence, or political instability are not eligible for refugee status and therefore lack protection from refoulement and are often denied the right to work, but we should not think that this exclusion is something natural to the definition of refugees. Other definitions have been used in national and international law. In the United States, for example, the 1965 Immigration and Nationality Act (the Hart-Celler Act) counted refugees as people who were persecuted, uprooted by natural disasters, fleeing communist countries, and fleeing the Middle East. After ratifying the 1967 UN Protocol, the United States moved to align its definition with the UN definition in the 1980 Refugee Act, thereby eliminating protection for those once classified as refugees for other reasons.[36] Other parts of the world retain a more robust definition of refugees. For example, in 1969, the Organization of African Unity (now the African Union) adopted the Convention Governing the Specific Aspects of Refugee Problems in Africa, which defines refugees as those who flee due to external aggression, occupation, foreign domination, or events seriously disturbing the public order. The

---

34 Gil Richard Musolf, "The Asylum-Seeking Process: An American Tradition," in *Conflict and Forced Migration: Escape from Oppression and Stories of Survival, Resilience, and Hope*, ed. Gil Richard Musolf (Bingley, UK: Emerald, 2019), 25.

35 Suzanne Monyak, "Garland Withdraws Asylum Limits for Domestic Abuse Victims," *Roll Call*, June 16, 2021, https://rollcall.com/2021/06/16/garland-withdraws -asylum-limits-for-domestic-abuse-victims/.

36 García, *Refugee Challenge*, 4–5.

gaps in coverage of nonconvention refugees are a result of the development of laws, which can be changed, but many nations currently lack the will to do so.

While Jesus, Mary, and Joseph would have no trouble meeting this second criterion (facing a pertinent category of persecution and qualifying for protection), there are many others who would fail to do so. To expand our consideration of biblical characters for a moment, Jeremiah, who (rather unwillingly) fled the Babylonian armies and escaped to Egypt (Jer 43:1–7), or Abraham, who fled from drought and famine (Gen 12:10), would probably be arrested and deported.

No Aid from One's Home Nation

The fourth criterion to qualify as a refugee (I will consider the third in the next chapter) is that a refugee "is unable, or owing to such fear [of persecution], unwilling to avail himself of the protection of [his or her] country" (Article 1 A). This is a reasonable stipulation that fits within a common Christian ethical principle known as subsidiarity, a principle that suggests that issues should be addressed at the lowest institutional level proportionate to the problem. Besides being a more efficient approach, lower institutional levels are more likely to have a direct relationship with the individual in need, explaining their duty of care. In this case, if a nation can provide protection for someone facing persecution—perhaps through an appeal to the police, perhaps through a legal system—then such protection must be sought prior to seeking international aid. Admittedly, this criterion is sometimes applied too heavy-handedly, as when some nations require that asylees "exhaust all reasonable domestic protection possibilities before asserting their entitlement to refugee status."[37] However, in principle, this is a reasonable feature of any definition of *refugee*.

Once again, Joseph and Mary satisfy this stipulation. Appealing directly to Herod and asking him to stop his persecution would be foolish and dangerous. One might attempt to appeal to Caesar, but this would also be unlikely to succeed. Herod had been given the title of "ally and friend" by Augustus Caesar, a designation of support that gave Herod extensive power.[38] Furthermore, the right of appeal to Caesar was restricted to Roman citizens (Acts 22:22–29 and 25:10–12 illustrate the benefits and rights of Roman citizenship).[39] Since neither Joseph nor Mary were citizens, they lacked even a basic avenue for appeal to Caesar, Herod's superior. Nor would they be likely to find support from some other powerful benefactor, since the patronage system of the Roman Empire resulted in benefactors helping those who could provide something in return.[40] There would be no help for the holy family in their homeland, so the international refugee regime rightly provides an alternative path to secure their lives, safety, and rights.

---

37 Nergis Canefe, "The Fragmented Nature of the International Refugee Regime and Its Consequences: A Comparative Analysis of the Applications of the 1951 Convention," in *Critical Issues in International Refugee Law: Strategies toward Interpretive Harmony*, ed. James C. Simeon (Cambridge: Cambridge University Press, 2010), 176.

38 Witherington, *New Testament History*, 58.

39 The Roman Empire did not automatically grant citizenship to residents within its borders. Rather, one became a citizen either by being born to a citizen father, by serving in the Roman army, or by being a family member of a Roman soldier. On one estimate, only 7 percent of individuals who lived in the empire yet beyond the Italian peninsula were citizens. See Derek Heater, *Brief History of Citizenship* (Edinburgh: Edinburgh University Press, 2004), 31, 35.

40 Roman patronage and benefaction tended to target communities, family, friends, and individuals with some influence. While a patron or benefactor would gain some prestige from helping one in need, generally, there was an expectation of public recognition in return, the sort that a migrant Judean family in Egypt would be unlikely to provide, even if they were able to find a potential patron or benefactor through their networks. See John Nicols, *Civic Patronage in the Roman Empire* (Leiden: Brill, 2013), 8–13.

The holy family meets three criteria for refugee status and receiving the protections and rights associated with it. They have a well-founded fear of persecution for one of the reasons stipulated by the 1951 Refugee Convention, and they are unable to seek protection from the country in which they reside. However, the situation is not so straightforward. While a person or persons count as refugees from the moment they meet relevant legal criteria, specific governments still must determine whether that refugee status will be recognized and all legal, economic, and political benefits conferred. Refugees must not only meet relevant criteria but be able to prove that they meet such criteria in court. This burden of legal proof will be the first of several hurdles that the holy family must overcome to receive protection under the 1951 Refugee Convention.

The Burden of Proof

The holy family would need to prove in court that they satisfy the criteria to qualify as refugees. If Jesus, Mary, and Joseph sought to prove this in the context of seeking asylum, having already crossed into another nation's territory without proper documents, failure to prove their case in court could result in incarceration and/or deportation, including a return to their homeland, where they would be within Herod's reach. If the holy family had instead arrived at a refugee camp, proving their refugee status would be a prerequisite to resettlement in another country. In both cases, the stakes are high with the holy family's life and freedom on the line.

Different standards of proof are needed in different contexts. Many are familiar with the standard of proof in US criminal law—to convict someone of a crime, their guilt must be proven "beyond a reasonable doubt." This is not the standard used in the determination of refugee cases. In the United States, the 1987 Supreme Court case *INS v. Cordoza-Fonseca* ruled that establishing "well-founded fear" was not based on the likelihood of persecution beyond a reasonable doubt. It even rejected a requirement of "clear probability" or proving persecution "reasonably likely to occur," which implied a probability of persecution being more likely than not.[41] In the court's words, "One can certainly have a well-founded fear of an event happening when there is less than a 50% chance of the occurrence taking place."[42] Instead, the threshold of proof was that of a "reasonable possibility"—if persecution is a genuine possibility, fear of this persecution is considered well founded in American law.

The European Union has worked to unify its asylum principles, policies, and procedures. The process is not yet complete and has taken years, and a degree of regional variance is still allowed and expected.[43] To simplify, I will focus on Germany to illustrate a different possible procedure. In Germany, there are two stages of evidentiary assessment. First is the establishment of facts, such as the individual's country of origin, other details about that individual, and broad facts about the country of origin. This stage requires evidence beyond a reasonable doubt. In a second stage, drawing on the facts, a prognosis of the risk of

---

41 Goodwin-Gill and McAdam, *The Refugee in International Law*, 57–58; Zimmermann and Mahler, "Article 1 A," 341.

42 Quoted in Zimmermann and Mahler, "Article 1 A," 341. Indeed, "US case law on the federal level demonstrates that a risk of around 10 per cent might be enough to have a well-founded fear of being persecuted. British and Canadian cases followed this approach" (342).

43 For a brief overview, see Ida Staffans, *Evidence in European Asylum Procedures* (Leiden: Martinus Nijhoff, 2012), 27–33. See also Vincent Chetail, "The Common European Asylum System: *Bric-à-brac* or System?," in *Reforming the Common European Asylum System: The New European Refugee Law*, ed. Vincent Chetail et al. (Leiden: Brill, 2016), 3–38.

future persecution is made—here, like in the United States, the standard of proof is a "reasonable likelihood."[44] Germany has also deployed the "reasonable person-test," asking "whether a reasonable observer would draw the conclusion from external facts that the person seeking refuge would be subject to persecution in his home country."[45]

With these standards in mind, we can begin to consider whether the holy family would be able to prove their refugee status in court. I am not a lawyer, and the full outcome of the trial would no doubt depend on technical procedures, precise legal precedents, and arguments that I am not qualified to make. Nevertheless, with the basic standards of proof in place and with literature on the broad sorts of facts often playing a decisive role in asylum trials, I can propose a basic assessment of Jesus, Mary, and Joseph's chances. Since we are performing a thought experiment for illustrative purposes anyway, this should suffice to understand the broad contours of the international refugee system. As we will see, within these broad parameters, there is good reason to worry that Jesus, Mary, and Joseph's refugee status would not be recognized. In fact, some historians have come to doubt Matthew's story for the same reasons that courts often doubt refugees' stories.

We should note that many details about Mary and Joseph's life might not be provable beyond a reasonable doubt, as is required in the first stage of the German procedure. Likely, in the haste of departing in the middle of the night, Joseph and Mary, like many refugees, would have forgotten evidence and documents that might verify parts of their story, such as the visit from the magi,

---

44 Staffans, *European Asylum Procedures*, 135–40.
45 Zimmermann and Mahler, "Article 1 A," 341.

for example. This visit is a key element in Joseph and Mary's case, for it proves that Herod might know of Jesus as a potential threat to the throne, thereby justifying the holy family's fear of persecution. The lack of such documentation means that if the holy family sought refuge in Germany, they might not be able to prove the magi's visit beyond a reasonable doubt, leaving the discussion of the magi (for example) inadmissible in the second stage of evidentiary assessment considering the acceptance or rejection of refugee status for the holy family.[46] Often, a lack of external corroboration can be fatal to a refugee's case. Similarly, some historians are skeptical of Matthew's narrative for its lack of external corroboration. Paula Fredriksen and E. P. Sanders both argue that the lack of extrabiblical attestation to the slaughter of children in Bethlehem by Herod (Matt 2:16) raises doubts about whether the events Matthew describes even occurred.[47] This lack of corroboration would likely prevent the holy family from appealing to Jesus's membership in the particular social group of children aged two and under, a group far too small to attract international attention, leading to doubts about the veracity of the risk. If the doubts are "reasonable," that might be the end of the holy family's chances for asylum in Germany.

Even in an American context, where the burden of proof is lower, discrepancies in the story might be sufficient to reject the petition for asylum. Often, courts look for discrepancies in stories to cast doubt upon refugees' narratives. David Bezmozgis, himself a refugee, recounts an incident where he served in solidarity with another refugee writer seeking asylum in Canada.

---

46 Ida Staffans explains that the merits of a claim for refugee status is "based only on the facts that have passed the [first] threshold." Staffans, *European Asylum Procedures*, 138.

47 Paula Fredriksen, *From Jesus to Christ: The Origins of the New Testament Image of Jesus* (New Haven, CT: Yale University Press, 2000), 37; E. P. Sanders, *The Historical Figure of Jesus* (London: Penguin, 1993), 87.

The asylum seeker's story was challenged at multiple points. Would a man fearing for his life remain at his parents' house waiting for papers for several weeks? If local police are a threat to his life due to his writing, could he not flee elsewhere? Bezmozgis notes that his friend's responses, which seemed so implausible to the court, are "the peculiar logic and idiosyncrasy of a human life—much of which could not be substantiated."[48] If a judge believes there are holes in a refugee's story, the requested asylum might be denied.

Historians are similarly skeptical of Matthew's account of the flight to Egypt due to discrepancies between Matthew's birth narrative and Luke's, which does not include the magi, the flight to Egypt, or Herod's massacre of the children of Bethlehem. Such scholars suspect that these discrepancies show that the holy family never actually fled to Egypt. Fleur Houston believes that there are too many parallels between Exodus's account of Moses and Matthew's narrative of the flight to Egypt, suggesting Matthew is inventing the narrative with an agenda. As she explains, Joseph, Jesus's earthly father, was led by dreams (Matt 1:20; 2:13, 19), as was Joseph, Jacob's son, who entered Egypt with the end result of Moses being born in Egypt (Gen 37:1–11; 40:1–41:40). Pharaoh ordered the death of all Hebrew boy babies, as did Herod (Matt 2:16). The death of Pharaoh (Exod 4:19–20) allows the return of Moses and beginning of Exodus, as the death of Herod allows the return of Christ (Matt 2:19).[49] Geza Vermes sees additional overlap between folk tales of Moses written much later than Exodus and Matthew's birth narratives.[50] The

48 David Bezmozgis, "Common Story," in *The Displaced: Refugee Writers on Refugee Lives*, ed. Viet Thanh Nguyen (New York: Abrams, 2018), 43–50.

49 Fleur S. Houston, *You Shall Love the Stranger as Yourself: The Bible, Refugees, and Asylum* (London: Routledge, 2015), 135.

50 Geza Vermes, *The Real Jesus: Then and Now* (Minneapolis: Fortress, 2010), 86.

coincidences are simply too convenient, leading many to doubt the truthfulness of Matthew's narrative.[51] In light of these parallels, E. P. Sanders thinks that Luke does not agree with Matthew that Jesus was a new Moses, so he does not include these stories whose agenda is to show Jesus in Mosaic light.[52] Neither historical account, though, is considered particularly accurate by these scholars. But what about the historical record that we have, which details the violent nature of Herod? Does this record count for anything in establishing the validity of the holy family's story? Marcus Borg and John Dominic Crossan explain, "The 'slaughter of innocents' is completely in character for the suspicious if not paranoid Herod. That, of course, simply proves that Matthew intends a realistic parable and not necessarily a factual history."[53]

We can see that the success of the holy family's recognition as refugees—which would guarantee their protection and right to work, move freely, and seek an education for Jesus—is quite precarious. Courts might doubt their narrative for the same reasons that some historians doubt Matthew's. In light of these possible objections, the largest determining factor would probably be the judge assigned to the case. As Rebecca Hamlin notes, "Even among asylum adjudicators in the same office who are considering applications from the same country of origin, acceptance rates can vary wildly, in some cases ranging from below 5 percent to above 80 percent."[54] In other words, the success of the holy family's case would likely depend primarily on the

51 See also Helen K. Bond, *The Historical Jesus: A Guide for the Perplexed* (London: Bloomsbury, 2012), 27; and Fredriksen, *From Jesus to Christ*, 37.

52 Sanders, *Historical Figure of Jesus*, 88.

53 Marcus Borg and John Dominic Crossan, *The First Christmas: What the Gospels Really Teach about Jesus's Birth* (New York: HarperOne, 1989), 145.

54 Rebecca Hamlin, "Ideology, International Law, and the INS: The Development of American Asylum Politics 1948–Present," *Polity* 47, no. 3 (July 2015): 334.

decision-maker who determined the outcome of their case—here again, the question of who is assigning refugee status matters.

The reflective reader might recognize one of the larger challenges of refugee policy: discrepancies in one's story could, in fact, be evidence of deceit. Surely, in the name of national security, we must make every effort to identify those who would seek to enter a country under false pretenses, right? This is a valid concern and one that will be addressed more extensively in chapter 5. For now, I can summarize by saying that the national security threat of asylees and refugees, or of immigrants more broadly, is relatively small. If a nation is concerned about national security, there are alternative means of providing for refugees and asylees that may soften these (mostly unwarranted) worries. Instead of pursuing these alternatives, most nations have preferred a method of deterrence, seeking to repel potential asylees, often by force. Though I recognize the concern some have about asylees, I ultimately do not find it compelling for two additional reasons. First, criminal background checks in various international databases seem to be a more effective way to identify security threats. Second, there is good evidence that expecting exhaustive, documented, detailed, and nonconflicting accounts from refugees is an unreasonable standard of evidence.

Psychological research has demonstrated that the sorts of inconsistencies sought in courts to disqualify asylees are inappropriate rubrics for discerning which asylees are telling the truth. Jane Herlihy, Laura Jobson, and Stuart Turner summarize, "The very basis of the asylum claim is an assumption that people can reliably, consistently and accurately recall autobiographical memories."[55]

---

55 Jane Herlihy et al., "Just Tell Us What Happened to You: Autobiographical Memory and Seeking Asylum," *Applied Cognitive Psychology* 26, no. 5 (September/October 2012): 662.

However, as Herlihy, Jobson, and Turner show, there are numerous problems with this assumption. For example, there is "considerable support" for the hypothesis that high levels of stress impede the ability to make correct identifications and have accurate memory. One study found that soldiers being trained through simulated high-stress interrogation had difficulty identifying their interrogator only twenty-four hours later.[56] In situations where stress is acute enough to lead to post-traumatic stress disorder (PTSD) or depression, conditions prominent among refugees, memory is even more seriously affected. PTSD has been shown in studies to result in sensory, perceptual, and emotional aspects of memory being more easily retrieved, while conceptual aspects necessary for testimony tend to be disrupted. Those with trauma, PTSD, and depression have been shown to have difficulty recalling specific autobiographical memories.[57] Consistency has become central in identifying a true account of an asylum seeker, but large studies of veterans have found that they changed basic details about their experiences over the period of several years.[58] Detailed recall is also undermined by PTSD.[59] Even in situations where departures do not produce PTSD or depression and are not even significantly stressful, memory can be a fickle thing. For example, studies of memory have shown that the order of cues for questions may affect what a person can remember.[60] In other words, families like Jesus, Mary, and Joseph often flee without time to secure proper documentation and evidence to prove aspects of their stories, and they often

---

56 Herlihy et al., 663–64.
57 Herlihy et al., 665–66.
58 Herlihy et al., 667.
59 Herlihy et al.
60 Herlihy et al., 663.

lack the physiological or psychological ability to recall the details of their escapes in the manner expected by courts.

Culture can also pose a challenge in the context of an immigration hearing. UNHCR guidelines on interviewing asylum seekers reveal how language barriers may cause problems, illustrating with the following story: "A Turkish asylum-seeker, applying for refugee status in Switzerland, stated that he had escaped arrest by hiding in mountains near his hometown. The application was rejected. Among the reasons given was the fact that the town was situated amid hills. For the Swiss interviewer there were no mountains in the region and thus the applicant was considered not credible. However, in Turkish, the term 'mountain' also applies to hilly regions."[61] Such cultural and linguistic differences are well known to the High Commissioner for Refugees, but such information might be unknown to a given lawyer or judge. As a result, inconsistencies or confusing aspects of stories that arise from differences in culture and language may be attributed to dishonesty on the part of the asylee, resulting in a state not recognizing the rights that individual is properly due. In short, judges frequently disqualify asylees from protection due to inconsistencies, vagueness, or confusing and illogical aspects of the asylee's narrative when these are precisely the sorts of features that we should expect from real asylees based on cultural differences and the psychological consequences of stress, trauma, and depression.

---

61 UNHCR, "Interviewing Applicants for Refugee Status (RLD 4)" as cited in Kelly Oliver, "Abolish Refugee Detention," in *Refugees Now: Rethinking Borders, Hospitality, and Citizenship*, ed. Kelly Oliver, Lisa M. Madura, and Sabeen Ahmed (London: Rowman & Littlefield, 2019), 123.

The Holy Family's Precarious Legal Case for Refugee Status

The holy family would qualify as refugees in terms of the three criteria explored so far. They have (1) a well-founded fear of persecution; (2) on the basis of religion, membership in a social group and/or political opinion; and (3) an unwillingness and inability to avail themselves of help from the government of their homeland. Yet there is reason to believe that they would have difficulty proving their case in an asylum hearing. Historians have raised objections to Matthew's narrative that mirror the sorts of objections raised against refugees by courts today, including a lack of corroborating evidence and inconsistency in the stories told, even though the field of psychology and general awareness of cultural differences both assure us that we should expect precisely these sorts of features in the narrative of an actual refugee.[62] Herod was a powerful and cruel leader, a genuine threat to his subjects and political opponents, and a source of frequent human rights violations. Even so, we already see ways in which our modern system might not provide protection for Jesus, Mary, and Joseph were they to hypothetically seek refuge under the modern international system. In addition, our exploration has shown many other nonconvention refugees—such as those fleeing war, natural disaster, or gender-based violence—would not be protected under the 1951 Refugee Convention, though some fraction of nonconvention refugees might find lesser protection under other statutes. Simply put, many vulnerable nonconvention refugees

---

62 I am not using these psychological studies to make an argument about the historicity of Matt 2, a topic beyond the scope of this work. Rather, I use historical criticism of Matt 2 as part of this thought experiment to illustrate exactly the types of skepticism the holy family would likely encounter in court.

whose lives are at risk may lack legal recourse to claim protection, instead facing incarceration and expulsion. At the end of chapter 2, then, we already see some weaknesses in the care provided by the current refugee regime. As we turn to chapter 3, we will consider the largest legal hurdle to the holy family's pursuit of refugee status, continuing to probe the current refugee system for gaps and weaknesses.

3

The Route to Safety

IF THE HOLY FAMILY TRAVELED the Way of Shur,[1] the most common route from Judea to Egypt, it would have taken them about forty-five days to reach Alexandria, the Egyptian city with the largest Jewish population in the first century. Traveling to Pelusium, the closest Egyptian city to Judea, would have taken roughly thirty days.[2] The holy family's destination was determined by God and declared by an angel in Matthew 2:13—"Flee to Egypt," the angel said, leaving little room for negotiating different possible destinations. This angelic proclamation is decisive for our thought experiment, since a flight to Egypt instead of to

---

1 This route is mentioned in Gen 16:7.
2 Benjamin A. Foreman, "Matthew's Birth Narrative: Matt 2:1–18," in *Lexham Geographic Commentary on the Gospels*, ed. Barry J. Beitzel and Kristopher A. Lyle (Bellingham, WA: Lexham, 2017), 26–27.

another location is the largest hurdle to the holy family being recognized as refugees. The fourth criterion for fitting the definition of a refugee according to the 1951 Refugee Convention and the 1967 Protocol is being "outside the country of [one's] nationality" (Article 1 A). Though there is some ambiguity, this criterion likely would disqualify Jesus, Mary, and Joseph from receiving protected status. Migration theory will help us explore the reasonableness of this fourth criterion, ultimately showing further weaknesses in the current international regime. Before turning to migration theory, though, it is necessary to consider an ambiguity in interpreting the flight to Egypt.

An Interpretative Ambiguity

The differences in the geopolitical situation between the first century and the twenty-first make it challenging to decide how to interpret the holy family's flight to Egypt from Judea. We might interpret their travel as migration from one Roman-occupied territory to another. Rome controlled Judea through the consistent presence of the Roman army. We might interpret the situation like the United States' involvement in Iraq or Afghanistan, for example. Though Afghanistan was occupied by the US military and controlled in many respects by the US government during the period from 2001 until 2021, Afghans were still eligible to apply for refugee status and asylum in the United States. So perhaps we should interpret the relationship between Judea and other parts of the Roman Empire similarly—the holy family could leave occupied Judea and seek asylum in other parts of the Roman Empire. However, the length of Roman control of Judea makes this interpretation implausible, as does the fact that Roman administrators and government officials had direct control over Judean affairs.

Perhaps the flight from Judea to Egypt is best interpreted as migration from one sovereign territory to another, where both territories are part of a larger transnational political entity. In this interpretation, the Roman Empire is something like the European Union, which is composed of individual sovereign states. In the European Union, migrants moving between EU member states are in some circumstances recognized to have the rights of refugees. For example, the European Court of Human Rights has ruled that in some circumstances, if an EU member state returns a migrant to the member state in which they entered the EU zone, this might violate the principle of nonrefoulement.[3] This interpretation might be plausible, since Herod had been given the title of "ally and friend" by Augustus Caesar. Ben Witherington summarizes that this is "in fact a legal status giving Herod virtually unlimited power and control as a client king over his own domain."[4] If Judea and Egypt were each a sovereign nation, then the holy family would certainly qualify as refugees, though again, their legal recognition as such would be somewhat in jeopardy based on a high burden of proof.

However, this interpretation of the historical situation has its problems. For one, unlike the European Union, client kings in the Roman Empire do not have the right to peaceably leave the Roman Empire, from which there was no Brexit. Another problem with this interpretation is that, unlike the situation in the EU, the client kings derive their authority from the centralized authority of the Roman Empire, whereas in the European

3 A law known as the Dublin Convention allows EU states to return migrants to the state in which they first entered the European Union, except in those circumstances ruled a violation of the principle of nonrefoulement by the European Court of Human Rights. Hemme Battjes, "A Balance between Fairness and Efficiency? The Directive on International Protection and the Dublin Regulation," *European Journal of Migration and Law* 4, no. 2 (April 2002): 159–60.

4 Witherington, *New Testament History*, 58.

Union, the inverse is the case: any central authority is conferred by member states.

The holy family's flight to Egypt is probably best interpreted as a move within the sovereign borders of the Roman Empire, their homeland and country of nationality. For this reason, like all migrants who flee danger but do not leave their homeland, the holy family would not count as refugees and therefore would not be due the legal protection accorded to refugees by the 1951 Refugee Convention. Instead, they would be classified as internally displaced persons, or IDPs for short.[5] This might seem like a quick end to the thought experiment that is central to this book, but ending this line of inquiry here would be premature. Several questions immediately present themselves, which must be further explored. First, why do migrants move to one location instead of another? In Joseph's case, he was directed to Egypt by an angel (Matt 2:13), but most refugees and IDPs are not guided in this manner. Might there be a good reason for an IDP not to flee beyond his or her homeland, one that should not eliminate their protection by the international community? Second, obviously, the 1951 Refugee Convention did not exist when Jesus, Mary, and Joseph fled to Egypt. Suppose they were seeking safety in our modern refugee regime. In that case, the angel might have directed them elsewhere.[6] Would the holy family have a realistic chance of crossing an international border

---

5 There is some debate about the viability of this category, since many persons who are not displaced may face similar human rights violations at home. See Walter Kälin, "Internal Displacement," in Fiddian-Qasmiyeh et al., *Oxford Handbook*, 166–67. For my part, I find the IDP a helpful concept, partly because those who are displaced are already on the move and hence more likely to become asylees and refugees.

6 Here, one might reply that the Messiah had been prophesied to come out of Egypt, so no other destination is possible, to which I might reply, hypothetically, that the prophecy might have been otherwise if modern refugee protection were available. Anyway, this is a thought experiment, so cut me some slack.

and thus of gaining the protection due to refugees? The rest of chapter 3 and chapter 4 will consider these questions.

Migration Routes and Migration Theory

If someone is facing persecution in the country of their nationality but lacking any means of securing safety in that homeland, they must leave their country in order to qualify as a refugee instead of being an IDP. This might lead us to ask why more IDPs do not just leave the country of their nationality to seek safety. One reason some IDPs do not leave their country is that other nation-states have security measures in place preventing them from doing so. However, security measures alone do not explain migration patterns. Migrants usually do not arbitrarily travel to a destination but choose among certain routes that are more feasible to them based on several factors. These basic factors help us understand broad features of the choices facing an IDP, refugee, or asylee (not to mention other immigrants), even though each individual or family makes choices that are also shaped by very personal factors. The study of migration theory can therefore help us begin to understand why some who face the risk of persecution are IDPs, while others are refugees.

Migration theory often considers push factors, which are reasons why a person might leave their country, and pull factors, reasons why a person might be drawn to a new location. Push factors may include the risk of persecution, natural disasters, or war and other violence. We cannot assume that any of these risks will automatically result in emigration; there are countless examples of citizens and IDPs who remain in their homeland despite facing violence or disasters. However, such sources of instability may raise the possibility of immigration to a family that has never

considered it before. Poverty is often assumed to be an important push factor that leads individuals to leave a country. However, there are reasons to think the relationship between poverty
and immigration may not be so straightforward. For example,
between 1965 and 1980, there was an increase in immigration
to the United States from Latin America, Asia, and the Caribbean, but for many countries of origin, this period was a time
of major economic growth.[7] In other words, while poverty was
declining, immigration was growing. This may be because the
poorest of the poor often lack the funds necessary to successfully
migrate.[8] In fact, the poorest nations tend to have low levels of
emigration.[9] On the other hand, it could also be that increased
emigration leads to more remittances (money sent home from
the new host country), fostering economic growth.[10] Emigration
may lead to economic growth, or economic growth may lead to
emigration. Likely, the relationship between poverty and emigration is quite complex and bidirectional. This is not to say that
the economy can never push migrants to leave,[11] but it is the case

---

7 "Annual GNP growth hovered around 5 to 9 percent for most of these countries [of origin]." Saskia Sassen, *The Mobility of Labor and Capital: A Study in the International Investment and Labor Flow* (Cambridge: Cambridge University Press, 1988), 14.

8 Migrants typically face either expensive visa application processes for legal avenues or expensive fees for smugglers to get across borders without such documents. Those without funds are typically much less likely to succeed at immigrating. A study by Cooray and Schneider found that in nations with heavy corruption, the poor were also less likely/able to emigrate, while wealthier and higher educated individuals were more likely to. See Arusha Cooray and Friedrich Schneider, "Does Corruption Promote Emigration? An Empirical Examination," *Journal of Population Economics* 29, no. 1 (January 2016): 293–310.

9 Tisha M. Rajendra, *Migrants and Citizens: Justice and Responsibility in the Ethics of Immigration* (Grand Rapids, MI: Eerdmans, 2017), 27.

10 This is the basic theoretical perspective analyzed by many of the essays in Nina Glick Schiller and Thomas Faist, eds., *Migration, Development, and Transnationalization: A Critical Stance* (New York: Berghahn, 2010).

11 Miguel De La Torre provides a helpful narrative of how Mexican migration to the United States increased as a result of NAFTA and US corn subsidies destroying the Mexican agricultural market. De La Torre, *Immigration Crisis*, 23–28. Even here, though, many of the pull factors I discuss momentarily were also an important factor.

that patterns of migration are not determined exclusively or even primarily by economic considerations.

Various pull factors draw immigration, though there are different ways to think about how such factors work. Tisha Rajendra divides theoretical analyses of pull factors into three groups: agency-dominant, structure-dominant, and migration-systems theories. Agency-dominant theories tend to consider the choices of individuals who are pursuing maximal utility, often expressed in economic terms. On this account, migrants are drawn to wherever they can earn the most money or enjoy the greatest job opportunities. Such approaches do not always fit the data well, Rajendra notes. They predict "that migration would occur any time wage differentials exist between two countries, and this is simply not the case."[12] Agency-dominant theories cannot explain why migrants choose one nation over another when faced with two possible destinations with better economic opportunities than migrants' countries of origin.[13] They also assume migrants are making choices when migrating, which is not the case for many "tied movers," individuals like children or (in some

---

12 Rajendra, *Migrants and Citizens*, 36. In defense of agency-dominant approaches, there are a restricted set of cases where the model is a better fit. In Puerto Rico, where migration to the mainland United States is not restricted legally, data fits neoclassical models much better, though still not without flaws. Factors beyond wages must be considered even where there is no legal barrier to migration. See Douglas S. Massey et al., "An Evaluation of International Migration Theory: The North American Case," *Population and Development Review* 20, no. 4 (December 1994): 702–5, 709. Even in Massey et al.'s survey of immigration studies in the 1970s, '80s, and early '90s, they admit that support for neoclassical theory must at least be supplemented by other theories: "International migration is not fully explained by wage gaps alone. At the most general level, countries with the lowest wages relative to those in the United States are not necessarily the largest senders of migrants; and even after wage differentials are controlled, significant variation in the aggregate volume or individual likelihood of emigration remains unexplained. Although migration decisions may be sensitive to international wage differentials, therefore, the accumulated empirical evidence suggests that they may not be the most important factor in determining migration decisions" (710).

13 Massey, "Evaluation of International Migration Theory," 37.

cultures) spouses who may not have a say in migration decisions.[14] Structure-dominant theories of migration consider "economic, social, political, and historical structures" to be the main causes of migratory patterns, typically considering how some form of exploitation or harm may lead to migration.[15] Such approaches acknowledge that migration patterns are shaped by forces larger than individual choice. However, they tend to minimize the agency of migrants and ignore the impact of decisions by businesses or political authorities in destination countries that may draw immigrants.[16] Neither of the first two theories adequately fit the available data.

Rajendra champions a third perspective, that of migration-systems theory, which "shows how both the agency of migrants and the structures of migration are crucial to understanding transnational migration."[17] The most important pull factor in this context is the establishment of a migration route through colonialism, government-sponsored labor recruitment, and/or foreign investment.[18] Each of these acts by a potential recipient country can establish transnational relationships. Once migrants enter a country when invited to work, they retain familial connections to relatives in their home country, communicating about their new homes. They also establish economic connections through remittances and new export/import channels, and they amplify a process of mutual cultural influence between the home and destination countries.[19] Each of these ties makes

---

14 For more on this subject, see Haines, *Immigration Structures*, 114–15.

15 Rajendra further subdivides this group into segmented-labor-market theory, historical-structural theory, and world-systems theory. For present purposes, the broad similarities of each suffice to make Rajendra's point. Rajendra, *Migrants and Citizens*, 42–43.

16 Rajendra, 44.

17 "Agency and structures both condition one another." Rajendra, 45.

18 Rajendra, 46.

19 Thomas Faist, Margit Fauser, and Eveline Reisenauer, *Transnational Migration* (Malden, MA: Polity, 2013), 27–45.

migration more realistic to a migrant, and empirical evidence confirms the influence of these ties on migration routes.[20]

The case of foreign financial investment is more complicated.[21] As Saskia Sassen explains, foreign investment in a country might result in migration for several reasons. First, the introduction of commercial farming and rising urban labor opportunities may push or pull subsistence farmers into urban wage-labor roles. Subsistence farmers may lose or sell their land, move to a city seeking a job, and then wind up without land or work if factories move to even cheaper labor markets. Because they are already disconnected from their communities of origin, such workers are more likely to emigrate. Second, economic development often creates new employment opportunities for women, sometimes even displacing men from the workforce, resulting in further emigration. Third, and perhaps most importantly, though, is the fact that direct investment establishes an objective link between the investing country and the country receiving investments.[22] Jobs created may cause increased language proficiency, making migration more feasible. As employees rise in the ranks of a foreign company, they may have the opportunity to immigrate to the home office, or else travel there briefly for training, developing cultural familiarity. These factors may encourage patterns of migration.

We ought not reduce migration patterns entirely to the choices made by immigrant-receiving countries and resulting migration routes. As Rajendra explains, migrants do make choices about

---

20 See the survey of evidence in Massey et al., "International Migration Theory," 729–33. Studies commonly find that over time, economic factors are replaced by transnational networks in the migration patterns of individuals who repeatedly migrate and in the migration patterns from entire countries.

21 "This is a highly mediated process, one wherein direct foreign investment is not a cause but a structure that creates certain conditions for emigration to emerge as an option." Sassen, *Mobility of Labor*, 20.

22 Sassen, 18–20.

where to move, but such choices are "conditioned" by the macrolevel migration patterns. At the same time, "the individual decisions of migrants and their families have an impact on and change the structures of migration."[23] We have been speaking so far of migration in general, but these trends are true of refugees as well. Each refugee will make decisions or will move as a tied mover with others who make decisions. Yes, the range of decisions available to refugees may be limited, but choice is rarely eliminated. Often, choices are shaped by existing migratory patterns—refugees might follow routes friends and relatives have already taken, travel to a safe location where they have heard work is available, or flee to a city where they know someone speaks their language. Refugee resettlement programs are generally an exception here, since there are far more refugees than available resettlement opportunities. Yet even here, there can be migratory patterns. Factors like which resettlement nonprofits have necessary language proficiencies might result in migration patterns where refugees of a particular nationality or ethnicity follow the routes their community members have already taken.[24]

Refugee migration often takes the form of a series of decisions made within certain structures and migration patterns such that it may be difficult to identify whether a country is a transitional or final stop. Heaven Crawley and Katharine Jones analyzed over five hundred interviews of Afghan, Syrian, and Nigerian refugees in Turkey, Italy, Greece, and Malta. A significant subset of these interviews involved individuals or families who made temporary stays in Turkey, Iran, and Libya before finally migrating to the European Union. Crawley and Jones

---

23 Rajendra, *Migrants and Citizens*, 47.

24 Stephan Bauman, Matthew Soerens, and Issam Smeir, *Seeking Refuge: On the Shores of the Global Refugee Crisis* (Chicago: Moody, 2016), 92–93.

found patterns like those discussed by migration-systems theory. Syrian Kurds and Turkmen, for example, often moved to Turkey because they had family connections and could speak the same language as some Turks.[25] Many refugees intended to stay in Turkey, Iran, and Libya but were eventually compelled to move farther into Europe. In Libya, the main push factor driving migration was violence (more on this next chapter). In Iran, the push factor was racial discrimination, especially against Afghan Hazaras.[26] In many instances, a refugee would first seek safety in Iran or Libya but later decide that discrimination or violence required further migration to European nations where the refugee might have connections. Multistage journeys can cause problems for refugees seeking recognition in European courts. Their initial flight might meet the criteria of a well-founded fear of persecution on the basis of race, religion, nationality, membership in a social group, or political opinion, but their departure from countries like Iran, Libya, or Turkey would not qualify. If the wrong part of their story is shared, they might be deemed nonconvention refugees and refouled to the violence of Libya or the racism of Iran. If their departure from their homeland was too long ago, they might be deemed to violate article 31 of the refugee convention, which requires asylees to present themselves "without delay" to authorities.

We see many of the pull factors discussed by migration-systems theory in the holy family's flight to Egypt. Jews had long been connected to Egypt through colonization from

---

25 Heaven Crawley and Katharine Jones, "Beyond Here and There: (Re)conceptualizing Migrant Journeys and the 'In-Between,'" *Journal of Ethnic and Migration Studies* 47, no. 14 (2021): 3233.

26 Crawley and Jones, 3235. In Iran, Afghans cannot drive cars or motorcycles, get a SIM card, or go to the flea market.

various empires that relocated and displaced Jews into Egypt.[27] Elephantine was home to a Jewish garrison of mercenaries and even boasted a temple until it was destroyed in 408 BCE.[28] The conquest of much of the Middle East by Alexander the Great and then by the Ptolemaic and Seleucid kingdoms that followed the collapse of his empire resulted in a common Greek language used in Egypt and Judea that would make migration feasible. Alexander himself welcomed Jewish settlements in Alexandria and gave Jewish communities in the city political rights and opportunities.[29] Various ruling powers over Egypt during several centuries BCE welcomed Jews to fulfill their labor needs. For example, evidence from burial inscriptions shows that Jewish mercenaries fought with Ptolemaic armies when the Ptolemies ruled Egypt.[30] Alexandria, like many cities in the Eastern Roman Empire, had a Jewish *politeuma*, evidence of the institutional possibilities open to Jews in Egypt under subsequent empires' rules. A *politeuma* was a well-established, autonomous, institutional community that sought legal protection for Jewish residents and funded cultural, religious, and architectural projects. They had their own courts and joined synagogues into a consolidated network. Egypt also had deep economic and social ties to Judea. Diaspora Jews paid an annual temple tithe to Jerusalem, which in some ways mirrors modern remittances paid by emigrants to families still in their homelands. Diaspora Jews also completed pilgrimages to Jerusalem, and we have records

---

27 I suspect that Israelite slavery in Egypt and Egyptian colonization of parts of Canaan in the thirteenth century BCE were too ancient to have any lingering effect on migratory patterns in the first century.

28 A concise treatment of this is found in Victor H. Matthews, *A Brief History of Ancient Israel* (Louisville, KY: Westminster John Knox, 2002), 120–22.

29 Foreman, "Birth Narrative," 26.

30 Eric S. Gruen, "Judaism in the Diaspora," in *Early Judaism: A Comprehensive Overview*, ed. John J. Collins and Daniel C. Harlow (Grand Rapids, MI: Eerdmans, 2012), 118.

of written communication between Egyptian Jews and Jewish communities in the Judean homeland.[31] Patterns of migration from Judea to Egypt were well established by the time of the flight to Egypt through colonial and imperial efforts to resettle Jewish populations in Egypt thanks to a desire for Jewish labor to serve as mercenaries and other professions.

The connections between Egypt and Judea indicate that, even without angelic instructions, it would have made sense for Joseph to lead his family to Egypt when seeking refuge. By way of comparison, we can see that established routes of migration farther west into the Roman Empire or east into the Parthian Empire would have been less likely. Jewish communities in the Western Roman Empire typically lacked the centralization of a *politeuma*, meaning that while they had the freedom to worship, they lacked the equivalent cultural and political influence of Jews in Egypt and were likely smaller communities.[32] The western parts of the Roman Empire also lacked the long history of imperial connections between Egypt and Judea, so there were likely more pull factors for the holy family in Egypt. For example, Greek was more frequently spoken in Egypt than in Iberia at the time, and where Egypt had played a central role in Jewish religious imagination, for better or worse, since the narratives of the Patriarchs—the Greek city Elephantine had once been so central to Jewish religious life that it boasted its own temple—the Jewish connection with the western parts of the Roman Empire lacked an equivalent religious and cultural link.

---

31 Gruen, 127–28. Gruen describes 2 Macc and the *Letter to Aristeas* with qualities that I might term *transnationalism*.
32 Shaye J. D. Cohen, *From the Maccabees to the Mishnah*, 2nd ed. (Louisville, KY: Westminster John Knox, 2006), 104–5.

When turning east to consider the Parthian Empire as a possible place of refuge for the holy family, we lack robust sources but have some reason to believe that there are smaller transnational relations between Judea and Parthia than between Judea and Alexandria.[33] When the Parthian Empire conquered Seleucia, it gained a significant Jewish population.[34] Jews in the Parthian Empire continued to make a pilgrimage to Jerusalem (see the list of peoples in Acts 2:9–11) and to pay the temple tithe.[35] There is also limited evidence of political negotiations between Herod and Parthian leaders.[36] Notably, Herod was able to secure the repatriation of his potential rival, John Hyrcanus, from the Parthians. (Hyrcanus was murdered shortly after this repatriation.)[37] Major Judean rabbis communicated to Babylonian Jews in the Parthian Empire by letter, and some notable first- and second-century Jewish religious figures may have spent time in Parthia.[38] However, the political organization of Jews in Alexandria was more advanced than that of Parthian Jews. Eventually, an exilarchate called the Resh Galuta provided a degree of self-governance to Jews in Babylonia, but there is no evidence

---

33 On the scarcity of sources, see Geoffrey Herman, "The Jews of Parthian Babylonia," in *The Parthian Empire and Its Religions: Studies in the Dynamics of Religious Diversity*, ed. Peter Wick and Markus Zehnder (Gutenberg, Germany: Computus Druck Satz and Verlag, 2012), 141–50.

34 Raoul McLaughlin, *The Roman Empire and the Silk Routes: The Ancient World Economy and the Empires of Parthia, Central Asia, and Han China* (Barnsley, UK: Pen & Sword, 2016), 152.

35 Gruen, "Judaism in the Diaspora," 128.

36 Jason M. Schlude and J. Andrew Overman, "Herod the Great: A Near Eastern Case Study in Roman-Parthian Politics," in *Arsacids, Romans and Local Elites: Cross-Cultural Interactions of the Parthian Empire*, ed. Jason Schlude and Benjamin Rubin (Oxford: Oxbow, 2017), 93–110.

37 Jacob Neusner, *A History of the Jews in Babylonia. I—The Parthian Period* (Leiden: Brill, 1969), 34.

38 Neusner, 39–41, 45.

of an effective exilarch in the first century.[39] Despite Josephus recounting the brief reign of a Jewish lord in Parthian territories, generally, Jews at the time seemed to lack political institutions, though mid-first-century reforms, perhaps under Parthian Vologases I, gave Jewish communities more political prominence.[40] One could speculate that this lack of political organization might also be reflected in weaker Jewish economic and religious institutions in Parthia as compared with Alexandria. Each of these areas indicates a stronger likelihood that the holy family would have deeper transnational ties with Egypt than with Parthia. Like most modern refugee families who settle in urban areas rather than camps or rural areas, it would not be surprising that the holy family proceeded to a city and, in this case, specifically to one like Alexandria in Egypt.

One reason IDPs might relocate within the country of their nationality, even when faced with persecution by their own government, is that they may lack clear connections to a transnational community with existing migration patterns that would facilitate an easy move beyond their homeland. When suddenly fleeing home and wondering who they can travel to for help, the immediate options could all be within their own country. Some IDPs, therefore, have needs as severe as refugees and asylees but networks that are more constricted. Perhaps with this in mind, European and North American nations have, at times, provided help to potential refugees before they leave their own country, though this is certainly not the norm. Such strategies show that the holy family would not be completely without hope of aid

---

39 An exilarchate is basically a Jewish patriarch for the exiles in Babylon. Neusner summarizes, "If an Exilarch existed before the end of the first century, he left no evidence of his influence and for all practical purposes one can hardly say that such an institution existed as an effective force" (*History of the Jews*, 53).
40 Neusner, 54–59.

even within the boundaries of the Roman Empire, their country of nationality. In US refugee law, which was last substantially updated in the Refugee Act of 1980, a refugee is "a person outside any country of such person's nationality" who has faced persecution or has a well-founded fear of persecution or else "any person who is within the country of such person's nationality" who faces such persecution *and* whom the president chooses to specify as a refugee.[41] Joseph and Mary could pursue such special presidential recognition as refugees to receive full protection, though success seems unlikely. IDPs are not typically recognized as refugees by US law, despite legal possibilities to the contrary.

In the last two decades, the European Union has shifted to emphasize "the protection of refugees in regions of origin." This policy involves both preventative actions outside the borders of the European Union to mitigate the causes of refugee displacement as well as efforts to establish safe zones to protect refugees either in their homeland or else in the region of their homeland in situations where they have fled beyond its borders. While such efforts have established regional safety zones outside of displaced populations' native lands, Emma Haddad argues that this externalized refugee policy has its unofficial origins in the safe zones established in response to displacements in Yugoslavia in the early 1990s and later in Kosovo in 1999, which sought a safe zone for displaced migrants within their national borders.[42] One of the main objectives of both policies has been to prevent flight into EU member nations by providing care external to the European Union.[43] These actions raise the possibility that the European Union would

---

41 Refugee Act of 1980, 8 U.S.C. § 1101 (a)(42)(A, B).
42 Haddad, *Refugee in International Society*, 178. Haddad notes that by the early 2000s, this emphasis was becoming a matter of official policy.
43 Haddad, 178, 181.

recognize a group of displaced migrants as candidates for refugee status but would seek to provide protection prior to the refugees reaching the borders of an EU member state. The holy family, if interpreted as IDPs, might receive EU protection within the borders of the Roman Empire. However, in these circumstances, such recognition would be highly unlikely as there would not be a large enough migratory group to draw the attention of authorities within the European Union. It would be exceedingly implausible that something like a safety zone would be established that would benefit Jesus, Mary, and Joseph.

Now that it is clear that the holy family would likely not receive protection under the 1951 Refugee Convention, even granting the (unlikely) possibility of recognition under the US Refugee Act of 1980 or protection by an EU safe zone, we can ask another question: Supposing the holy family knew that protection as a refugee was a possibility, would they be able to successfully enter a country outside of the Roman Empire and claim asylum? Unfortunately, their odds of success here are low.

"Illegal" Immigration, International Law, and Refugees

Under the current definition, refugees must be outside of the borders of the country of their nationality to receive any protection, while IDPs receive less care from the international community. This dilemma incentivizes would-be refugees to cross international borders without permission or documentation, the only feasible means of securing refugee status. An asylee could not seek safety from a potential host nation's embassy within the asylee's homeland, because most nations do not permit asylum petitions at their embassies.[44] They are unlikely to be able to fly to a potential host country, because most potential host nations deny access to travelers with passports from nation-states prone to refugee displacement. Airlines can be fined for transporting anyone with a passport from such origin points, so typically, travelers are also screened by airline employees and prevented from flying to a state where they might seek asylum.[45] To prevent flights to neighboring regions and subsequent border crossings, the United States, Canada, and Mexico coordinate their responses such that if a refugee cannot fly to the United States, they are unlikely to be able to fly to Canada or Mexico either.[46] Since short-term travel is prohibited, a potential asylee might be tempted to gain entry through another immigration category (maybe a student visa or an employment-based immigration visa), but applications for other immigration venues are far too slow to be a feasible means of reaching safety. Herod would have killed Jesus before the necessary bureaucratic processes were completed. Admittedly, some short-term migrants may enter a state lawfully only to later become refugees—in such circumstances, they are still protected from prosecution if their papers expire—but this is not a common route to refugee protection.[47]

Perhaps anticipating how many doors would be closed to refugees, the drafters of the 1951 Refugee Convention expected and intended refugees to make undocumented border crossings.[48] Article 31 of the 1951 Refugee Convention prohibits the

44 David Scott Fitzgerald, *Refuge beyond Reach: How Rich Democracies Repel Asylum Seekers* (Oxford: Oxford University Press, 2019), 2.
45 Fitzgerald, 7–8, 63–65.
46 Fitzgerald, 61–65.
47 Gregor Noll, "Article 31," in Zimmermann et al., *1951 Convention*, 1258.
48 This is one reason the terminology *undocumented immigrant* is preferable to *illegal immigrant*—many who are undocumented are following the expectations of international law.

punishment of refugees making undocumented border crossings, provided the refugees making such crossings (a) come directly from a country where they are at risk and (b) apply promptly. Requirement (a) allows for traveling through states other than a refugee's homeland that are still unsafe. "Directly" was also interpreted by the drafters to allow a brief time of transit through unsafe and even safe states to the ultimate destination.[49] However, the expectation was that many would move to cross borders without documentation in a relatively quick time frame and that this was to be permitted. As we will see in chapter 4, many states put considerable effort into ensuring that refugees cannot enter at all without documentation, or at least not without great expense, delay, and difficulty. Because of this, most refugees and asylees must rely on smugglers, and article 31 does not protect such smugglers from prosecution, even if they are bringing refugees across a border, which, by international law, refugees have the right to cross.[50] This situation is one of many reasons why some smugglers are connected with criminal networks.

Though undocumented border crossings were expected by the framers of the 1951 Refugee Convention, many commentators today object to the requirement that refugees be outside of the country of their nationality. There are several reasons to object to this provision. First, in the words of Thomas Gammeltoft-Hansen, "it would seem illogical that the refugee who succeeds in crossing the border illegally would enjoy greater protection than the refugee who lawfully presents him- or

---

49 Goodwin-Gill and McAdam, *Refugee in International Law*, 264–67. This does not mean that refugees who do not come directly from their homeland can be refouled to their homeland as provided for in article 33 of the 1951 convention, but it does mean that they are not protected from prosecution under article 31 paragraph 1. Noll, "Article 31," 1254.
50 Noll, "Article 31," 1253.

her-self to authorities at the border."[51] As we will see in the next chapter, those who are intercepted outside of a nation's borders and who request asylum are often denied asylum hearings, while those who enter illegally—and the word *illegal* is vague here, since entry may be legal by international law but prohibited by domestic law—are protected from refoulement. Second, asylum procedures for undocumented refugees are sometimes unclear. The United States, for example, lacked any clear procedure for such cases for the first thirty years of the 1951 Refugee Convention's existence.[52] Third, the division between "internally" and "externally" displaced persons may be difficult to maintain in practice. For example, the breakup of Yugoslavia was underway while the genocide in Bosnia and Herzegovina occurred, making it challenging to identify when migrants were IDPs or refugees.[53] Such factors led many to conclude that the division between IDPs and refugees confuses and prevents care of the most vulnerable rather than enabling it.[54] Others argue that the recipient nation is intended as a "surrogate," fulfilling the role of the country of nationality. When an IDP is still within their country, full surrogate responsibilities are impossible and, perhaps, unneeded.[55] I do not intend to fully resolve this debate here, but the fact that the holy family remained within the Roman Empire and so likely would not receive protection as refugees does not automatically mean that they should not receive such protections.

---

51 Thomas Gammeltoft-Hansen, *Access to Asylum: International Refugee Law and the Globalisation of Migration Control* (Cambridge: Cambridge University Press, 2011), 45.

52 Vernon M. Briggs Jr., *Mass Immigration and the National Interest* (Armonk, NY: M. E. Sharpe, 1992), 128.

53 García, *Refugee Challenge*, 85.

54 For example, see Haddad, *Refugee in International Society*, 26–27.

55 This argument is explained in Canefe, "Fragmented Nature," 175.

Borders and Safety

Jesus, Mary, and Joseph fled to Egypt, a flight that followed an established migratory path rooted in deep transnational connections and a flight that also would lead, in our thought experiment, to their lacking the full protection afforded to refugees under the 1951 Refugee Convention. In this chapter, I have explained how the route chosen by many displaced and persecuted persons may be based on what relationships they have abroad because of transnational communities and migration routes typically established by earlier colonization, labor programs, or foreign investment. Therefore, it is concerning that IDPs often lack the protection available to refugees, the provisions of the Refugee Act of 1980 in US immigration law notwithstanding. I have also shown that if the holy family hypothetically wanted to pursue the protections available under the modern refugee regime, they would need to cross an international border without permission or documentation. This necessity certainly complicates many criticisms of undocumented immigration and many policies designed to prevent such immigration. As we will see in chapter 4, both the United States and the European Union have gone to extreme lengths to ensure that potential refugees and asylees like Jesus, Mary, and Joseph cannot cross the very borders that they are expected to cross to find safety. If the holy family had faced persecution by Herod in the context of the modern refugee regime, they, like millions of other modern families, would have been faced with a difficult choice. Either they could remain IDPs without international protection, risking arrest and return to face persecution and execution, or they could pursue asylum and refugee recognition by crossing a militarized international border. We turn now to consider the risk facing refugees hoping to cross borders.

4

Crossing Dangerous Borders

ONE OF THE MOST STRIKING features of the story of the holy family's flight to Egypt is how little there is to it. The text tells us that the holy family "stayed there until the death of Herod" (Matt 2:15), after which time, "the angel of the Lord appeared in a dream to Joseph in exile and said, 'Rise, take the child and his mother and go to the land of Israel, for those who sought the child's life are dead'" (Matt 2:19b–20). While there are stories of Christ's life that are not preserved in the Gospels (note John 20:30), apparently nothing happened in Egypt that was so noteworthy as to be included in Matthew's narrative. Jesus, Mary, and Joseph's uneventful arrival and stay in Egypt stands in stark contrast with the typical experience of many modern refugees who face years of delay in squalid refugee camps or while squatting in urban settings or else attempt to cross borders and to seek asylum, likely meeting violent measures by states and individuals along the way and deprivation of due process upon requesting asylum in a host nation. Asylum measures are so complicated that many simply remain undocumented immigrants in urban areas, a possibility foreign to the first century.

The ease with which the holy family entered Egypt was the result of the Roman conquests of both Judaea and North Africa. The ancient Near East had a long history of borders, sometimes fluid but sometimes with a relatively stable sense of distinct nations and territories.[1] Since a mass migration from Canaan to Egypt in roughly 3000 BCE, Egypt had slowly built a defensive perimeter to prevent invasion, a perimeter that relied not only on walls and crocodile-infested canals but also on natural barriers like waterless deserts and marshlands with quicksand. At times, the Egyptians paid or offered tax exemptions to northern Bedouin, who might serve as border scouts in some ways analogous to border patrol.[2] Rome, too, would establish border security, using a series of *burgi*, fortified towers with small garrisons.[3] From the standpoint of Rome, however, the border between Judaea and Egypt did not require the same degree of fortification, since movement between various parts of the empire was much less securitized during the *pax Romana* and given that even borders at the limits of the Roman Empire were not as clearly set in Africa as in parts of Europe.[4] The holy family likely took

---

1 Steven Grosby, "Borders, Territory and Nationality in the Ancient Near East and Armenia," *Journal of the Economic and Social History of the Orient* 40, no. 1 (1997): 1–29.

2 Ellen Morris, "Prevention through Deterrence along Egypt's Northeastern Border: Or the Politics of a Weaponized Desert," *Journal of Eastern Mediterranean Archaeology & Heritage Studies* 5, no. 2 (2017): 133–47.

3 Roger S. Bagnall, "Army and Police in Roman Upper Egypt," *Journal of the American Research Center in Egypt* 14 (1977): 71–73.

4 Guy Halsall, *Barbarian Migrations and the Roman West 376–568* (Cambridge: Cambridge University Press, 2007), 140.

advantage of Roman-maintained roads to make their journey to safety. Were they to seek refuge today, their journey would likely be more perilous, and safety would require a considerably longer wait.

The Delays of Refugee Resettlement

Were the holy family to flee in the modern era, they would face the same two routes to safety that most modern refugees face. They might choose to pursue asylum by entering a country and then petitioning for recognition as refugees, hoping to obtain the right to economic, political, and social participation that refugee status permits while also securing a refugee's protection from refoulement. Alternatively, they might enter a host country and register with the United Nations High Commissioner for Refugees (UNHCR), residing in a refugee camp where the UNHCR, local governments, and various nongovernmental organizations would provide for their needs or squatting somewhere in an urban setting while they await resettlement in a host nation by the UN or repatriation to their homeland once it is safe to return. These paths are the ideal outcomes anticipated by the 1951 Refugee Convention. However, as we will see, the reality is far bleaker.

After World War I, many refugees returned home after only a few years, so it was conceivable at the time of the drafting of the 1951 Refugee Convention that this pattern could be the normal refugee experience.[5] This is far from the case today, when only 2 percent of refugees find homes each year through resettlement

---

5 For the example of Belgian refugees, see Gatrell, *Modern Refugee*, 47.

or repatriation.[6] Serena Parekh explores this dire situation in her examination of the global refugee regime, showing how refugees spend an average of twelve years waiting in camps that are designed to isolate them from the local population and prevent competition in the job market. (The average refugee spends seventeen years as a refugee—twenty-five if fleeing from war—but gives up on camp life after twelve years, probably to move illegally to urban areas.) Refugee camps are often like prisons in design, emphasizing "vision and control"—the restriction of exit from the camp combined with the ability to observe what is happening in the camps.[7] Like prisons, such camps are also fraught with violence. After the 1994 Rwandan genocide, an estimated six hundred people a day died from violence, disease, and starvation in refugee camps.[8] Investigation has uncovered routinized sexual violence against women in camps with local police often unwilling to investigate or actively involved in the atrocities.[9] Such violence is exacerbated by poor facilities; a lack of locking latrines for women; the necessity of long walks in the dark to collect food, water, or firewood from remote locations; and a lack of lighting within the camps, which are all factors contributing to increases in sexual assault.[10] Facilities are lacking in other ways too. The Dunkirk camp in France hosts three thousand refugees in tents battling rat infestation with access to only two water taps.[11] If Jesus's birth in a stable is common fodder for Christmas sermons on the need for hospitality, I can only

---

6 Parekh, *No Refuge*, 3.
7 Parekh, 5, 107–15.
8 García, *Refugee Challenge*, 103.
9 Agnés Callamard, "Refugee Women: A Gendered and Political Analysis of the Refugee Experience," in *Refugees: Perspectives on the Experience of Forced Migration*, ed. Alastair Ager (London: Pinter, 1999), 205, 109–10. Callamard specifically considers camps in Kenya, Djibouti, and Zaire, though other works explore similar dynamics elsewhere.
10 Callamard, 206.
11 Oliver, "Abolish Refugee Detention," 119.

64

imagine the sermons we would hear if the holy family's stay in Egypt was similar to the experiences of modern refugees. Yet since we do not see the Messiah himself as thirsty or his mother assaulted in Dunkirk, sermons about refugee lodging are, in my experience, quite rare.

What leads to such extended stays in refugee camps? Serena Parekh explains that four factors result in a situation of systemic injustice where most refugees are left in a situation where no one claims the duty to protect their rights (more on this in chapter 6). First, states have the right to determine who can and cannot enter their territory.[12] Individually, nonparticipation in refugee resettlement may not pose a problem, but collectively, the world's nation-states resettle only 1 percent of the refugee population each year.[13] Only 29 countries of 149 refugee convention signatories provided refugee resettlement in 2019.[14] Even the United States, which is typically the world leader in resettlement, though notably not during the Donald Trump administration, only resettles refugees who go above the bar of persecution and are of "special humanitarian concern."[15] Second, states have decided to rely on refugee camps, even though they are more expensive than alternatives and less likely to secure the legal rights of refugees.[16] Third, states tend to pursue policies to protect their citizens at the expense of refugees. Often, this stance is taken in the name of national security, protecting the poor working class, or the right to self-determination.[17] As

---

12 Though some seeking refugee reform seek to eliminate borders altogether, I remain in agreement with ethicists like Parekh who see a continued positive role for international borders. Arguing for this is beyond the scope of this work.

13 Parekh, *No Refuge*, 165–66. An additional 1 percent is repatriated each year.

14 Mark R. Glanville and Luke Glanville, *Refuge Reimagined: Biblical Kinship in Global Politics* (Downers Grove, IL: InterVarsity Academic, 2021), 221.

15 Parekh, *No Refuge*, 32.

16 Parekh, 166.

17 See chap. 5 for more discussion.

a result, refugees in camps are prohibited from working or traveling, and many governments rely on deterrence measures to prevent refugees from entering and seeking asylum. As we will see in chapter 5, the concerns about national security and the economic harm caused by refugees are overblown. Fourth and finally, Parekh notes that the 1951 Refugee Convention did not include any obligatory funding for the UNHCR, with each state left to determine its funding level. As states pursue their domestic fiscal goals first, the UNHCR is chronically underfunded.[18] Parekh summarizes the result: "The outcome is that the majority of refugees are structurally prevented from accessing refuge and the minimum conditions of human dignity."[19]

If Jesus, Mary, and Joseph escaped Herod and sought safety in a refugee camp, they would almost certainly fail to find any opportunities for resettlement, employment, or even formal education for the young Christ. While Matthew tells us that the holy family was apparently able to return within a short time frame to Judea after the death of Herod (Matt 2:19–21),[20] they would leave behind new acquaintances who would likely still have years of time remaining as refugees. Under such circumstances, one can see why many refugees attempt to enter states and seek asylum or simply seek jobs as undocumented workers. Perhaps the holy family, were they hypothetically fleeing Herod in the modern world, might pursue the course of asylum if they had heard of the terrible conditions of refugee camps. We have already considered what an asylum hearing might look like, but this assumes that the holy family had successfully entered a state

---

18 Parekh, *No Refuge*, 167.
19 Parekh, 168.
20 Note that Joseph is instructed to return with the child to Judea, suggesting time spent as a refugee is less than the seventeen-year average.

and filed for asylum. Successful border crossings, however, are not to be taken for granted, since most modern states that would be targets of refugee migration have taken extreme measures of militarizing their border patrols to prevent such entry.

Militarized Border Control and the Quest for Safety

Europe and the United States face a growing number of immigrants, both asylees and those commonly called economic migrants. As a result, each region has adopted a strategy of militarizing its border patrol to prevent the entry of immigrants. Some methods of deterrence act indirectly by seeking to eliminate pull factors that bring immigrants to a destination country. For example, stricter punishments for employers who employ undocumented immigrants might cause fewer companies to hire immigrants, drying up jobs and deterring immigration. Though such indirect methods of deterrence are important to consider, in this chapter, I want to restrict my analysis to a more direct, militarized prevention of migration. Since the word *deterrence* is reserved for indirect methods in much of the literature on immigration, I will speak of the militarization of border control, intending to refer to the intentional use of force on the border by government-sponsored individuals who draw on tactics, technology, and training commonly used in the military to deter and prevent immigrants from entering a nation-state.

Militarized border control (primarily the US Border Patrol in the United States and a variety of state agencies and Frontex, the joint EU border control, in the European Union) can use several kinds of violence, but in this section, I will focus on three. First, they might use direct force. Second, by threat of force, they might redirect migrants to points of danger, indirectly causing violence and loss of life. Third, they might threaten violent punishment or detention for immigrant infractions.[21] As we will see, all three methods are deployed across EU and US borders (and beyond). Such threats of force and violence can be accompanied using militarized personnel, equipment, and tactics. In 2010, for example, 28.8 percent of US Border Patrol agents were veterans of wars in Afghanistan and Iraq.[22] They were equipped with military technology like predator drones and armored personnel carriers. The United States has also directly deployed the military on the US border in "Operation Jumpstart" (2006—6,000 troops under President George W. Bush), "Operation Phalanx" (2011—1,200 troops under President Obama), and "Operation Strong Safety" (2014—1,000 troops under Texas governor Rick Perry).[23] The US military base in Guantanamo, Cuba, has been surrounded by land mines and barbed wire to prevent Cubans from crossing into American territory and seeking asylum.[24]

The Direct Use of Force

Often, immigrants crossing the border without documents, as asylees do by design in modern international refugee law, face the direct use of force with drastic consequences. Sometimes this

---

21 Reece Jones, *Violent Borders: Refugees and the Right to Move* (London: Verso, 2016), 10. Jones also refers to exclusion from the economy and damage to the ecosystem as violence, both important questions but both largely beyond the scope of this chapter and/or work.

22 Jones, 35.

23 Jones, 41.

24 The mines are technically Cuban, but Cuba and the United States have coordinated efforts to reduce Cuban asylum seekers from approaching the United States, and I am aware of no American objections to this buildup. See Fitzgerald, *Refuge beyond Reach*, 112.

is sanctioned. One of the worst instances of the sanctioned use of force against asylees occurred in Honduras on May 14, 1980, when four thousand Salvadorans attempted to flee across the Sumpul River into Honduras to avoid the Salvadoran army. In defiance of the 1951 Refugee Convention's prohibition against refoulement, the Honduran military turned them back at gunpoint, resulting in six hundred people quickly being murdered by the Salvadoran army.[25] Unsanctioned violence is also common. There are frequent reports of US Border Patrol agents acting cruelly toward detainees, forcing them to run long distances in the heat of the desert, kicking any who stopped, or releasing detainees who were stripped to their underwear into the near freezing night.[26] At times, Border Patrol agents kill unarmed migrants, like Dario Miranda Valenzuela, who was shot in the back, or Anastasio Hernandez Rojas, who was beaten and tased to death by over a dozen Border Patrol agents while handcuffed.[27] Though these acts are unsanctioned and others in the Border Patrol act professionally and do not commit such acts, these acts of violence are more common than many Americans would care to admit. At times, the use of violent methods is public knowledge. Greek police assault undocumented immigrants so frequently that "the European court of Human Right ruled in January 2011 that returning an asylum seeker to that country under the provisions of the Dublin Convention would expose them to

---

25 María Christina García, *Seeking Refuge*, 37.
26 A fuller account of the former is in Miguel De La Torre, *Trails of Hope and Terror: Testimonies on Immigration* (Maryknoll, NY: Orbis, 2009), 109. The latter example is recorded in Peter Eichstaedt, *Dangerous Divide: Peril and Promise on the US-Mexico Border* (Chicago: Lawrence Hill, 2014), 196.
27 De La Torre, *Immigration Crisis*, 13, 78–79.

torture, inhuman or degrading treatment."[28] At other times, violence is only discovered after investigation, as when it was found that in the 1980s, the Immigration and Naturalization Service (INS) committed violence against immigrants by tranquilizing them before forcing them to sign a voluntary deportation form.[29] Indeed, violence comes in many forms at the border.

At times, border violence escalates to the point of being a series of skirmishes. Consider the example of Melilla and Ceuta. In the autumn of 2005, migrants developed a new strategy to attempt to scale the fences around Spain's two African cities. Rushing the fences with ladders in groups of up to several hundred, they hoped that they could simply outnumber and overwhelm the Moroccan police and Spanish Guardia Civil and enter the cities, where they could pursue asylum or else seek a smuggler to bring them into mainland Europe by crossing the Strait of Gibraltar. The result was a series of skirmishes with injuries on both sides and the death of fourteen migrants. On the night of August 28–29, over three hundred migrants attempted a mass crossing, resulting in at least three migrants and ten Guardia Civil being wounded with two migrants dying, though the cause of death was disputed (some blaming rubber bullets, others claiming that a fall was responsible). Many more skirmishes occurred over the following month. One skirmish on September 28 resulted in thirty injuries to police and migrants; another on the night of September 29–30 resulted in two migrant deaths from barbed wire cuts and gunshot wounds and even the death of a baby when her Senegalese mother fell while trying to scale

---

28 Leanne Webber and Sharon Pickering, *Globalization and Borders: Death at the Global Frontier* (New York: Palgrave Macmillan, 2011), 100. The Dublin Convention allows EU member states to return asylees to the first European nation in which they traveled and to require them to apply for asylum there.

29 García, *Seeking Refuge*, 91.

the fence. Fourteen migrants died between September and October 2005 until the Spanish military arrived, and the new strategy was abandoned by potential asylees.[30]

Keep in mind that the explicit expectation in refugee policy is that many will cross a border without documents, which is legally permitted by international refugee law and the national law of many states. However, to successfully pursue this expected course, many asylees have to battle their way into a nation. This is not to say that all the individuals attempting to scale the fence at Melilla, for example, were refugees. But it does mean that if the holy family sought to flee Herod northward into Europe, where they would cross through Greece, or else to continue westward after Egypt with a goal of seeking asylum in Spain, they would likely face violent opposition. When undertaking this thought experiment, I see the young Jesus when I hear of the Senegalese baby who died in Melilla in 2005.

Violence and the Redirection of Migrants to Points of Danger

As the easiest geographic points of entry are militarized, migratory routes are redirected to dangerous points. After security increases in Arizona and in California, there was a correlated increase in deaths in dangerous border zones like the Arizonan desert and the All-America Canal in California.[31] As Weber and Pickering explain, "In the US, official Border Patrol statistics record a total of 4,375 deaths along the US-Mexico border

---

30 Sarah Léonard and Christian Kaunert, *Refugees, Security, and the European Union* (London: Routledge, 2019), 112–13.
31 Webber and Pickering, *Globalization and Borders*, 102.

from 1998 to 2009."[32] This count is generally assumed to be low because it only includes bodies found by Border Patrol (excluding bodies recovered by other agencies and persons reported missing) and excludes the Tohono O'odham nation, which is outside of Border Patrol's jurisdiction. Mexican authorities, relying on reports of missing persons not heard from after an attempted border crossing, suggest the real number is 300 percent higher.[33] In Europe, migratory routes were redirected to longer sea crossings, dangerous terrain, or more rarely, across old minefields. Counts of migrant casualties vary here as well. By one count, almost 14,000 migrants died between 1993 and 2010; of these, almost 10,000 drowned, 864 starved, and 73 died of land mines (among other causes).[34] Some other counts are far higher, with one claiming 23,700 migrants died due to EU militarized border control from 2005 to 2014.[35] In one much publicized 2013 tragedy, an overpacked smuggler's ship capsized near Lampedusa (a small Italian island), and over 350 drowned.[36]

We might be tempted to view such deaths as an accidental and unanticipated result of necessary increases in border security.[37] Weber and Pickering disagree: "Border deaths, far from being random and unforeseen events, are significantly shaped by particular border policies and practices that have both local inflection and global significance."[38] Though these deaths may have been unforeseen early in the process of building up border security (and this possibility is debatable), the consequences of

---

32 Webber and Pickering, 42–43.
33 Webber and Pickering, 43, 47–48.
34 Webber and Pickering, 1, 40.
35 Jones, *Violent Borders*, 16.
36 See the account in Jones, 18.
37 As we will see next chapter, the security threat associated with immigrants, including undocumented immigrants and asylees, is often overblown.
38 Webber and Pickering, *Globalization and Borders*, 91.

such policies are now clear. Yet both the European Union and the United States maintain their current course. In the European Union, this is manifest in proposed or enacted policies that restrict rescue operations for migrant vessels. As explained by one British Foreign Ministry official, "We do not support planned search and rescue operations in the Mediterranean" because they are "an unintended 'pull factor,' encouraging more migrants to attempt the dangerous sea crossing and thereby leading to more tragic and unnecessary deaths."[39] As a result, some European citizens who have attempted planned rescue operations have been charged with crimes.[40]

The danger of redirection is a function not only of geography but also of human agency. As terrain is more difficult to cross and borders are increasingly militarized, many asylees and other migrants must rely on a network of smugglers to enter a country. The results can be disastrous. At times, the negligence of smugglers increases migrant death. For example, in June 2000, fifty-four men and four women from the Fujian Province of China suffocated in a truck trailer while attempting an illegal entry. The Dutch smuggler, who was charged with manslaughter, had closed the air vent in an attempt to avoid detection through checkpoints.[41] Similar mass suffocations have occurred every few years in the United States and Europe. At other times, smugglers are partly culpable for the deaths of migrants as a result of their policy of leaving behind those who cannot keep up or by lying to

---

39 Jones, *Violent Borders*, 24.

40 For example, see Danielle Vella, *Dying to Live: Stories from Refugees on the Road to Freedom* (Lanham, MD: Rowman & Littlefield, 2020), 62–65. Vella recounts the Maltese prosecution of Claus-Peter Reisch after rescuing two hundred refugees at sea and refusing to turn them over to the Libyan Coast Guard, which would return them to the risk of slavery, kidnapping, torture, and in the best-case scenario, poverty and social exclusion.

41 Webber and Pickering, *Globalization and Borders*, 109.

migrants and telling them the four-day hike from the border to Tucson is only one day long.[42] Consider the example of Josseline Jamileth Hernández, a fourteen-year-old Salvadorian who began to vomit one cold night while walking with a coyote and other migrants through a desert canyon. The group had a ride to meet, so the coyote left her, assuring her that Border Patrol would soon find her. She was found, three weeks later, dead in the same canyon.[43]

Smugglers also commit or help others commit acts of violence toward those they are transporting across borders. In one incident, US Border Patrol found a man tied to a tree in the desert. If he had not been seen by helicopter, he would have died.[44] Many women crossing the southern border into the United States take birth control for months in advance due to the high likelihood of sexual assault along the journey.[45] Smugglers are also accused of setting their clients up to be robbed. A survey of deported migrants in Nogales, Mexico, found that one in five had been a victim of crime, robbed by bandits while trying to cross the border. Some were also kidnapped until they could pay a ransom.[46] Ransom by smugglers is a common, lucrative practice, causing many gangs to seek to control the border-smuggling industry. By one count, eleven thousand migrants were kidnapped in Mexico in only six months in 2010.[47] Extortion is often the smallest problem that kidnapped migrants face. Sometimes kidnappers and smugglers simply kill captives who

42 Margaret Regan, *The Death of Josseline: Immigration Stories from the Arizona-Mexico Borderlands* (Boston: Beacon, 2010), 57.
43 Regan, xi–xvii.
44 Eichstaedt, *Dangerous Divide*, 193.
45 De La Torre, *Trails of Hope*, 90; Fitzgerald, *Refuge beyond Reach*, 154.
46 Jeremy Slack and Scott Whiteford, "Violence and Migration on the Arizona-Sonora Border," in Slack et al., *Shadow of the Wall*, 52–53.
47 Jones, *Violent Borders*, 45.

are unable to pay, as when the Zetas, a Mexican gang, murdered seventy-two migrants in August 2010.[48]

Danielle Vella tells the story of a refugee named Amadou to illustrate the grisly nature of the smuggling industry in Libya. Amadou fled from Guinea toward North Africa, hoping to get across the Mediterranean. Along the route, he was unlawfully imprisoned by the Libyan smugglers he had hired to help him enter Europe. The smugglers asked him to call his family to seek a ransom. If the ransom wasn't paid on time, prisoners were tortured. Amadou shares, "They got a drill and they drilled a man's hands in front of my eyes. They pierced it. They forced him to dial the number of his relatives and they showed them. This made me cry, I tell you. I was so afraid." There are at least thirty known Libyan prisons of this sort that regularly house thousands of refugees.[49] If Joseph and Mary sought to enter Europe by boat across the Mediterranean, they would likely need to depart from Libya and rely on a smuggler, risking similar piercings much like the gruesome fate that, unknown to them, awaited their son.

Immigrant Detention

Though the 1951 Refugee Convention allows for brief detention of an asylee who crosses borders without documentation or permission, the expectation was that once the process of submitting a petition for asylum began, the asylee would be released, except under extreme circumstances like times of war where national security may require more extensive screening.[50] Despite this,

---

48 Fitzgerald, *Refuge beyond Reach*, 153–54.
49 Vella, *Dying to Live*, 51–55.
50 Daniel Wilsher, *Immigration Detention: Law, History, and Politics* (Cambridge: Cambridge University Press, 2011), 129.

refugee detention has increased dramatically, and in the 1980s, the United States began to use mandatory detention of Cuban, Haitian, Salvadorian, and other asylees until such a time as they are granted asylum at the end of a long legal process.[51] In 1996, the Antiterrorism and Effective Death Penalty Act (AEDPA) and the Illegal Immigration Reform and Immigrant Responsibility Act (IIRAIRA) mandated detention for certain categories of undocumented immigrants, broadening the trend of the 1980s.[52] Today, detention for immigrants has dramatically increased. Dominique DuBois Gilliard summarizes the situation in the United States with two pieces of data. Between 1990 and 2000, "arrests for immigration offenses increased 610 percent." By 2014, "61 percent of all federal arrests—over 100,000—occurred in just five federal judicial districts along the US-Mexico border."[53] Ostensibly, such detention might be defended as a means of ensuring asylum applicants do not run from future court hearings and remain in the United States as undocumented. However, there are alternatives to allow for asylum, avoid undocumented parolees fleeing into hiding within the United States, and avoid detention, which the US government has opted not to pursue, such as processing asylum applications in embassies. Worries about asylees skipping hearings does not alone explain the high use of detention.

Refugees face harsh circumstances in detention. Many of these detainees are placed in for-profit private prisons that force

51 Wilsher, 132–34. As Wilsher documents, the UNHCR interpreted American and European acts to be contrary to the 1951 convention.

52 Wesley Kendall, *From Gulag to Guantanamo: Political, Social and Economic Evolutions of Mass Incarceration* (London: Rowman & Littlefield, 2016), 88. The same laws brought about expedited removal, through which immigration officials could expel an undocumented immigrant without requiring a judicial hearing, another denial of due process for asylees (90–91).

53 Dominique DuBois Gilliard, *Rethinking Incarceration: Advocating for Justice That Restores* (Downers Grove, IL: InterVarsity Academic, 2018), 64–65.

immigrants to work for $1 a day.[54] A study involving nearly thirteen thousand interviews of immigrants detained by Border Patrol found that "only 20 percent of people in custody for more than two days received one meal. Children were more likely than adults to be denied water or given insufficient water."[55] Sexual violence is also common in some locations. For example, there were 170 complaints of sexual assault in four years against the privately run Broward Transitional Center in Florida, to name only one detention facility mixing refugees and criminal immigrants.[56] Though the United States has a long history of separating immigrant families in detention, the Donald Trump administration implemented a zero-tolerance policy requiring detention of all apprehended undocumented border crossers, including families, who had traditionally been paroled. When combined with a judicial ruling from the time of the Obama administration requiring expedited processing of children, this zero-tolerance policy resulted in at least 3,913 children being separated from their parents starting in 2017. Four years after the policy's implementation, the parents of 391 separated children had not been identified or reached, leaving many children in the US foster system.[57] Such could be the fate of a young Jesus if the holy family crossed the southern American border seeking asylum.

54 Gilliard, 66–67.

55 De La Torre, *Immigration Crisis*, 92.

56 Kendall, *From Gulag to Guantanamo*, 94.

57 Elliot Spagat, "US Identifies 3,900 Children Separated at Border under Trump," *Associated Press News*, June 8, 2021, https://apnews.com/article/az-state-wire-donald-trump-immigration-lifestyle-government-and-politics-54e2e5bbff270019d8bda3c81161c7c7.

A Lack of Due Process

Though the 1951 Refugee Convention and many domestic laws (e.g., the Refugee Act of 1980 in the United States) offer protection to asylees and refugees meeting the standard definition of a refugee, many nations deny asylees adequate opportunities to prove their status in courts. This denial of due process occurs across the globe but has been a staple of American immigration policy for at least the last half century. When I speak of a denial of due process, I am referring to legal procedures that deny either the stated rights of asylees and refugees or procedures that make it improbable or impossible for refugees and asylees to exercise their stated rights. While the most egregious example of a denial of due process to asylees is a program known as Operation Streamline, the United States has a long history of other policies designed to reduce asylees' likelihood of gaining asylum. To illustrate, I will begin with the example of Haitian refugees, a case that also illustrates the other principles discussed in this chapter.

Haitian Refugees: A Case Study

Denial of due process is frequently used to supplement strategies of militarizing the border control to prevent refugees from receiving protection within a country. Though there are many historical instances of denying due process, I will begin by focusing on US policy toward Haitian refugees in the 1970s through the 2000s. Chapter 3 explained the many factors that lead to specific migration patterns. I focused on Tisha Rajendra's argument that migration-systems theory offers the best explanation of migratory patterns by emphasizing how the economic or foreign policy of a nation may initiate migration patterns that are not easily stopped. Such is the case with Haitian immigration to the United States.[58] In 1915, the United States began a military occupation of Haiti with the intent to stabilize the country and to protect American and French interests in Haiti after a violent coup d'état.[59] As part of this occupation, the United States helped secure the election of a pro-American president who promptly gave the United States control of Haiti's foreign debt and established a US-trained military force that ruled by martial law.[60] When the Haitian General Assembly balked at the American demand of establishing a constitution that removed the long-standing Haitian ban on foreign property ownership (a request intended to open Haiti to American business interests), the US military helped disband the assembly, essentially establishing a dictatorship.[61] US-controlled Haitian presidents remained in power until the United States formally withdrew in 1934 after a period of protests and riots from Haitians who desired to be free of colonial control.[62]

---

58 The correlation between US involvement in Haiti, particularly during the Duvalier regimes, and immigration is explained in Lisa Konczal and Alex Stepik, "Haiti," in *The New Americans: A Guide to Immigration since 1965*, ed. Mary C. Waters et al. (Cambridge, MA: Harvard University Press, 2007), 447.

59 Haiti had been characterized by a long series of coups with limited casualties but considerable social instability for roughly a century, but the 1915 overthrow of President Guillaume Sam was particularly gruesome. Max Boot, *The Savage Wars of Peace: Small Wars and the Rise of American Power* (New York: Basic Books, 2002), 156–59. Secretary of State Robert Lansing explained that the military action was "to terminate the appalling conditions of anarchy, savagery, and oppression which had been prevalent in Haiti for decades" and "to forestall any attempt by a foreign power to obtain a foothold on the territory of an American nation." The latter objective was a response to fears of German military action in light of a probable Haitian default on German-held debt. See Boot, 160.

60 Malissia Lennox, "Refugees, Racism, and Reparations: A Critique of the United States' Haitian Immigration Policy," *Stanford Law Review* 45, no. 3 (February 1993): 693–94. US military captain Edward Beach summoned Dr. Rosalvo Bobo, the revolutionary poised to take power, and notified him, "You are not a candidate [for Haitian president] because the United States forbids it." Boot, *Savage Wars*, 161.

61 Boot, *Savage Wars*, 166.

62 Lennox, "Refugees, Racism, and Reparations," 695.

Informally, the United States retained power far longer, controlling the Haitian treasury until 1947 and supporting the election of President Francois Duvalier in 1957.[63] Francois and his son Jean-Claude Duvalier committed numerous human rights violations and murdered between twenty and fifty thousand of their citizens,[64] but as María Christina García explains, "The Duvaliers' anticommunist and probusiness orientation made them important US allies in the Caribbean, and few demands were made until ever-escalating migration from Haiti created a crisis for the United States."[65] Though ties were formally severed with Duvalier for a brief period beginning in 1963, the United States continued to provide him with military assistance until 1969.[66] By the early 1970s, diplomatic ties and economic support were official again, lasting until Jean-Claude left power in 1986.[67] When Jean-Bertrand Aristide, the first truly democratically elected president, was ousted by the military in 1991, it was the Duvaliers' American-supported private army, the *Tonton Macoutes*, who was responsible.[68] Harassment, assassination, arbitrary arrest, and other rights abuses continued into the 1990s.[69] This history provides a glimpse of the deeper ethical issues of immigration, which I will address more extensively in chapter 6. Not only had the United States established a relational basis for migration from Haiti to the United States, but

---

63 Lennox, 696.
64 Patrick Bellegarde-Smith, "Dynastic Dictatorship: The Duvalier Years, 1957–1986," in *Haitian History: New Perspectives*, ed. Alyssa Goldstein Sepinwall (New York: Taylor & Francis, 2013), 274.
65 García, *Refugee Challenge*, 48.
66 Lennox, "Refugees, Racism, and Reparations," 697. Lennox notes that even in 1971, a US warship was sent to help ensure the smooth transition of power from "Pappa Doc" Duvalier to "Baby Doc" Duvalier, his son.
67 Lennox, 697.
68 Lennox, 698.
69 Lennox, 706–7.

it arguably was also at least partly responsible for the political instability that characterized Haiti in the 1900s, creating a further duty to accept Haitian refugees. Despite this, considerable effort by a series of presidents attempted to prevent successful Haitian asylum hearings.

Though part of the American response to Haitian refugees involved intercepting boats and returning them to Haiti,[70] one of the primary means of preventing successful Haitian asylum petitions was to deny Haitians due process. In the 1970s, during the Nixon, Ford, and Carter administrations, the INS had been given guidelines that would nearly guarantee the failure of any Haitian asylum petition. Malissia Lennox summarizes, "The INS instructed immigration judges to increase their case load from as little as one scheduled deportation hearing a day to fifty-five hearings a day. Asylum interviews were shortened from an hour and a half to only fifteen minutes of substantive dialogue."[71] Such short hearings would make proving refugee status tremendously difficult. In addition, Haitians interdicted on the sea were given "interviews" to see whether they were eligible for asylum, but no lawyers were present.[72] It is therefore not surprising that of the roughly fifty thousand Haitian asylum applications from 1972 until 1980, only twenty-five were successful.[73] In a significant court case, *Haitian Refugee Center v. Civiletti* (1980), a judge ruled that programs targeting Haitians "resulted in wholesale violations of due process and only Haitians were affected."[74] Several weeks before this ruling, Jimmy Carter had established

70 For more on this, see García, *Refugee Challenge*, 50.
71 Lennox, "Refugees, Racism, and Reparations," 700.
72 Paul Lehmann, "Haitian Refugees," in *Immigrants, Refugees, and U.S. Policy*, ed. Grant S. McClellan (New York: H. W. Wilson, 1981), 89.
73 Lennox, "Refugees, Racism, and Reparations," 700.
74 García, *Refugee Challenge*, 50.

the temporary status of "Cuban-Haitian Entrant (Status Pending)," which suspended policies of deterrence and allowed boats full of refugees from both Caribbean islands to enter the United States and seek refuge. Briefly, it seemed as if the situation would improve for Haitians, but with the election of Ronald Reagan in 1980, policies of deterrence for Haiti were soon reestablished.[75]

The 1980s, 1990s, and 2000s were marked by a denial of due process for Haitian asylees. Under a 1981 accord with Haiti, the US Coast Guard began to intercept boats of Haitian refugees and return them to Haiti.[76] From 1981 until 1991, 23,551 Haitians were intercepted by the Coast Guard and returned to their country, while only 28 were allowed to apply for asylum with only eight receiving it.[77] In 1992, the George H. W. Bush administration adopted a similar policy, forcibly refouling Haitians who were typically disqualified based on a five-minute INS interview without access to legal counsel or not interviewed at all.[78] Beginning in 1981 under a new INS policy, Haitian asylees were no longer paroled (released into the United States while asylum proceedings were pending) but remained in detention where they were prohibited from meeting with a lawyer, a fact that greatly decreased their chances for a successful asylum petition.[79] This policy was eventually overturned in court, but the policy of deterrence by Coast Guard interception of Haitian boats ultimately survived legal challenges, with the Supreme Court eventually ruling in the 1990s that article 33 of the 1951 Refugee Protocol did not prohibit deterrence and refoulement outside of a

75 Briggs, *Mass Immigration*, 132.
76 García, *Refugee Challenge*, 50.
77 García, 50; Briggs, *Mass Immigration*, 133.
78 Lennox, "Refugees, Racism, and Reparations," 705, 718.
79 Lennox, 701. On the reduced chance of an asylum petition, see Fitzgerald, *Refuge beyond Reach*, 45.

signatory nation's borders.[80] In 2004 during the George W. Bush administration, the Coast Guard identified potential asylees by the unscientific "shout test"—only those apprehended in boats who loudly shout and get the attention of Coast Guard personnel are even considered for a possible asylum screening. David Scott Fitzgerald summarizes the results: "Of the 905 Haitians intercepted by the Coast Guard in February 2004, only three passed the shout test, and they were rejected by the 'credible fear' test onboard the cutter."[81] Currently, there is a resurgence in denial of due process to Haitian asylum seekers as the Biden administration has deported record numbers of Haitians, often under the controversial Title 42 program, which allows rapid deportation on the basis of alleged public health concerns during the Covid-19 pandemic.[82]

Contemporary commentators often compared Haitian and Cuban asylees. Apart from the brief status of Cuban-Haitian Entrant (Status Pending) in 1980, the two groups were treated in wildly different ways despite similarities in the broad political circumstances of both nations. While eight Haitians were granted asylum from 1981 until 1991, eight thousand Cubans received the status between 1988 and 1991 alone.[83] US presidents, members of Congress, and government officials had a vested interest in highlighting refugees fleeing communist Cuba during the Cold War, one factor in higher rates of Cuban acceptance. Another significant factor is likely that while most Haitian asylees were

---

80 The intricacies of these legal battles are a bit convoluted, but the basic contours can be discerned in García, *Refugee Challenge*, 58; Briggs, *Mass Immigration*, 132; and Lennox, "Refugees, Racism, and Reparations," 702–3.
81 Fitzgerald, *Refuge beyond Reach*, 90–91.
82 Eileen Sullivan, "U.S. Accelerated Expulsion of Haitian Migrants in May," *New York Times*, June 9, 2022, https://www.nytimes.com/2022/06/09/us/politics/haiti-migrants-biden.html.
83 Briggs, *Mass Immigration*, 133.

Black, few Cubans were. Allegations of racial discrimination or bigotry as a factor in denial of Haitian due process were common throughout the era, and while they were never able to be proven in court, it is difficult to interpret the evidence without some appeal to racial discrimination as a factor.[84] What is indisputable is that the US government intentionally denied legal representation, prevented asylum hearings, and expedited such hearings to the point of rendering them ineffective, resulting in a nearly complete denial of the right to seek asylum for Haitians. In short, in terms of our thought experiment, if the holy family were Haitian, it would be virtually guaranteed that they would not be recognized as refugees, regardless of the merits of their case. While the treatment of Haitians is particularly troubling, this denial of due process is common in US immigration practice. The Jewish holy family would still likely face immense hurdles in terms of obtaining due process were they to hypothetically seek asylum in the United States. To illustrate the other types of problems they might face, I will now explore the more recent policy known as Operation Streamline.

---

84 On historic claims of racism, see Briggs, 132; and García, *Refugee Challenge*, 52–53. Though undoubtedly, part of the preferential treatment of Cubans is due to the American desire to use refugees from a communist nation as a public example of the weaknesses of communism, this rational alone cannot explain the treatment of Haitians, who were the only group of asylees systematically denied parole, or why Haitians who did settle in Florida experienced frequent instances of bigotry. Konczal and Stepik, "Haiti," 448, 452. Even when compared to Guatemalans and Salvadorans, who had a much lower acceptance rate than Cubans (just under 3 percent in 1984), the acceptance rate was still nearly one hundred times that of Haitians from the same decade (0.03 percent). For Guatemalan and Salvadorean numbers, see De La Torre, *Immigration Crisis*, 116.

Operation Streamline

Operation Streamline is a federal policy requiring criminal prosecution of all who cross the border, an innovation compared to earlier policies. Previously in US law, first-time offenders without criminal records were simply deported, and the guidelines of the 1951 Refugee Convention severely restrict the use of detention against potential asylees. Because high levels of criminal prosecution resulted in a backlog of cases, there was a need to "streamline" the judicial process by trying offenders in groups of up to eighty detainees concurrently in a single trial.[85] The program was piloted in 2005 in Del Rio, Texas, during the George W. Bush administration but subsequently expanded to Tucson and Yuma, Arizona; Las Cruces, New Mexico; El Paso, Laredo, McAllen, and Brownsville, Texas; and San Diego, California.[86] The program has continued during the Obama, Trump, and Biden administrations.

Witnesses of the proceedings of Operation Streamline provide similar narratives.[87] When the proceedings begin, dozens of captive migrants shuffle into the courtroom, shackled, their peculiar shuffle a result of the fact that they have had their shoelaces taken while in custody to prevent suicide attempts. Migrants are sorted into groups and meet with attorneys or, sometimes,

---

85 Prosecution numbers are twenty daily on average in El Paso but up to eighty daily in Del Rio, Texas. Joanna Lydgate, "Assembly-Line Justice: A Review of Operation Streamline" (Berkeley, CA: Chief Justice Earl Warren Institute on Race, Ethnicity & Diversity, 2010), 4.
86 Lydgate, 1–3.
87 De La Torre, *Immigration Crisis*, 88–99; Tom Barry, *Border Wars* (Cambridge, MA: MIT Press, 2011), 25–30; Charles D. Thompson Jr., *Border Odyssey: Travels along the U.S./Mexico Divide* (Austin: University of Texas Press, 2015), 220–25. De La Torre viewed sixty-seven migrants processed in one day in Tucson, Arizona; Barry witnessed about seventy in Del Rio, Texas in 2009; Thompson observed seventy-five individuals processed in Tucson, Arizona.

paralegals. These meetings happen in groups or, quite rapidly, between an individual and their counsel. Given limited time, most work to describe the situations that led them to flee their homelands, but few reach an understanding of their legal rights or responsibilities, and even fewer can understand the complexities of the legal process they would need to navigate to secure asylum. After spending a quite brief time with their appointed lawyer, immigrants plead guilty in groups in front of the judge without a chance to share evidence. One observer timed the process he witnessed and found that if the total time spent on the official hearing was divided among the number of migrants present, the average time per migrant was 20.4 seconds.[88] Another witness tells how paralegals had helped some migrants prepare a two-sentence defense.[89] A third describes how a judge gave each detainee the opportunity to make a direct plea, though without legal consult, these were little more than a sentimental formality—as presented, these remarks had little legal significance.[90] These trials are among the most publicly observable results of efforts at enhanced enforcement or zero tolerance along the southern US border.

At one level, Operation Streamline can be seen as a method of deterrence by securitization, criminalization, and force like those methods discussed earlier in the chapter. The average detention period for those arraigned under Operation Streamline is 30 days, with some incarcerated for up to 180 days.[91] Time in prison is itself intended as a deterrence to illegal border crossings, but the effect of criminalization is further amplified by two

88 De La Torre, *Immigration Crisis*, 98.
89 Barry, *Border Wars*, 25.
90 Thompson, *Border Odyssey*, 223.
91 Lydgate, "Assembly-Line Justice," 12.

factors: first, individuals with a criminal immigration violation are prohibited from applying for legal venues of reentry to the country, including asylum, for up to ten years after the offense,[92] and second, individuals with misdemeanor immigration crimes who are caught making an illegal border crossing then face more serious felony immigration charges.[93] While studies have found that immigrants processed through Operation Streamline do not report higher levels of physical abuse or confiscation of property than other means of processing (and such violence is certainly still present), statistical analysis uncovered a higher rate of family separation for undocumented families processed through the program even before Donald Trump normalized the process of family separation.[94] In the words of one man who was unable to find his wife after she was processed through a different Operation Streamline trial than he was, "¡Te mata psicologicamente! (It kills you psychologically!)"[95] Operation Streamline is an egregious example of the denial of due process combined with elevated sentencing intended to deter border crossings.

As we will see below, immigration violations in the United States are typically treated as a civil offense, and defendants in civil trials do not have the right to a court-appointed attorney. Though Operation Streamline results in much higher levels of

---

92 Musolf, "Asylum-Seeking Process," 25. The extent of the restriction depends on how long an undocumented immigrant was in the country without authorization. Those facing expedited removal are barred for five years from reentry for any reason.

93 Jennifer M. Chacón, "Overcriminalizing Immigration," *Journal of Criminal Law and Criminology* 102, no. 3 (Summer 2012): 637–38. Chacón notes the continual rise in felony immigration charges, especially during the Obama administration.

94 The study found that Operation Streamline was linked to a 9.1 percent increase in likelihood of family separation. This is also not to say that physical abuse is not present in Operation Streamline, merely that it is no more present here than elsewhere in the US immigration system. Catalina Amuendo-Dorantes and Susan Pozo, "On the Intended and Unintended Consequences of Enhanced U.S. Border and Interior Immigration Enforcement: Evidence from Mexican Deportees," *Demography* 51, no. 6 (December 2014): 2255–79.

95 Slack and Whiteford, "Violence and Migration," 55.

detention and criminalization, one would at least hope that the transition to criminal offenses under Operation Streamline would result in better legal representation, since criminal procedures require the court appointment of an attorney if individuals lack their own representation.[96] Unfortunately, Operation Streamline has denied that due process to immigrants processed through the program. The average attorney-client meeting in Del Rio, Texas, is a few minutes, since trials may include up to eighty other individuals; in El Paso, with average caseloads of twenty per day, clients get about a half hour with their attorney.[97] When Christian ethicist Miguel De La Torre witnessed these trials in person, he described them as follows: "The court-assigned attorney meets with the defendants for the first time, usually in groups, to explain complex legal procedures in a few minutes, procedures that took me (a fluent English speaker with a doctorate) almost half a day to comprehend."[98] Not surprisingly, then, studies have found that most immigrants processed through Operation Streamline do not have a real opportunity to make a case for defensive asylum. In interviews with migrants, researchers at the University of Arizona found that

> when asked, "What did your lawyer inform you about your rights?" only thirty percent mentioned any sort of basic legal right such as the right to silence or a fair trial. Fifty-five percent of respondents stated that their lawyer simply informed them that they needed to sign their order

---

96 Many immigration offenses are treated as civil offenses, which do not include guaranteed representation. Criminal charges, however, do include the right to an appointed attorney if the defendant does not have the means or desire to secure legal representation on their own.
97 Lydgate, "Assembly-Line Justice," 13.
98 De La Torre, *Immigration Crisis*, 95.

of removal and plead guilty. Six percent reported that their lawyer did not tell them anything. Only one percent reported being informed that they could report abuses. And only three people stated that their lawyer screened for legal immigration options based on family connections, which is relevant to the subsequent removal process.[99]

When immigrants processed through Operation Streamline are presented with documents to sign pleading guilty, 99 percent do so,[100] even though 29 percent later admit they have no idea what they signed, and 28 percent claim to have felt pressure to sign.[101] Some argue that Operation Streamline is intended for more serious cases, like those who are caught with drugs crossing the border, but it does not appear that the program is restricted to such cases.[102] The Federal Rule of Criminal Procedure 11 states that due process requires that the court address the defendant personally, ensures the defendant understands constitutional rights, and determines a voluntary plea—standards of due process clearly not met through Operation Streamline.[103] As a result, the Ninth Circuit court eventually ruled prohibiting mass trials in Tucson, but other districts were not so restrained. Many who qualify for asylum under US and international refugee law never get to make their case, and even some who already have legal standing in the United States have been deported under Operation Streamline.[104]

---

99 Jeremy Slack et al., "In Harm's Way: Family Separation, Immigration Enforcement Programs, and Security on the U.S.-Mexico Border," in Slack et al., *Shadow of the Wall*, 79–80.
100 Lydgate, "Assembly-Line Justice," 3–4.
101 De La Torre, *Immigration Crisis*, 95.
102 See the reporting in Eichstaedt, *Dangerous Divide*.
103 Lydgate, "Assembly-Line Justice," 13–14.
104 Lydgate, 14.

Other Denials of Due Process

The denial of due process seen in Operation Streamline is typical of US immigration policy since at least the middle of the twentieth century. In 1981, the Reagan administration began to require undocumented immigrants to prove their refugee status defensively, meaning that migrants were jailed pending a formal hearing for asylum status. Failure to establish this status in court resulted in deportation.[105] Studies have shown that individuals who are incarcerated leading up to their trial have a far more difficult time in court due to restrictions on their abilities to meet with lawyers and obtain documentation or evidence.[106] Moreover, since many immigration violations are considered not criminal offenses but civil ones, "this means that detained aliens are not entitled to constitutional protections that are afforded criminals," including the right to an attorney.[107] Most immigrants have limited financial resources, so they must rely on pro bono (unpaid) legal representation. Without such representation, it is doubtful that asylees could successfully demonstrate a well-founded fear of persecution as outlined in chapter 2 or even know that this was the standard they needed to prove. Lack of legal representation in civil trials is a problematic aspect of counting immigration trials as civil law, but sometimes access to legal counsel is more intentionally prevented. In the 1981 case *Noe Castillo Núñez, et al., v. Hal Boldin, et al.*, Salvadorans and Guatemalans detained in Los Fresnos, Texas, sued after being denied the right to meet with legal counsel for legal proceedings.

---

105 Aristide R. Zolberg, *A Nation by Design: Immigration Policy in the Fashioning of America* (Cambridge, MA: Harvard University Press, 2006), 399.

106 For example, see Ellen A. Donnelly and John M. MacDonald, "The Downstream Effects of Bail and Pretrial Detention on Racial Disparities in Incarceration," *Journal of Criminal Law and Criminology* 108, no. 4 (2018): 775–814.

107 Amstutz, *Just Immigration*, 44.

The court issued an injunction in January 1982 "prohibiting the INS from denying detainees their rights."[108] Investigations in the United States found evidence that in the 1980s, INS used tranquilizers before pressuring detainees into signing the I-274A form that gave up their right to legal counsel and a deportation hearing, resulting in immediate deportation.[109] It is no wonder, then, that defensive cases are less than half as likely as affirmative hearings to win asylum.[110]

Though fights about due process were well underway in the early years of the Reagan administration, a consistent pattern of denying due process for asylees has continued in the United States ever since. For example, in 1996 during the Clinton administration, the IIRAIRA allowed expedited removal (without trial) for those lacking identification documents, but refugees often are unable to obtain such documents from their government or else flee in a rush while forgetting to grab their identification.[111] Under such policies, if Joseph and Mary forgot their documentation during their midnight departure (Matt 2:14), they would never even have the chance to apply for asylum.

Following the 9/11 terrorist attacks, a denial of due process began more systematically to target Muslims. Many Middle Eastern and South Asian individuals arrested on alleged immigration violations were tried in courts closed to the press where judges could see information that the detainees or lawyers could not even see to rebut.[112] The Patriot Act passed during the Bush administration allowed immigrants to be detained for a week without being charged with a crime or violation unless

---

108 García, *Seeking Refuge*, 108–9.
109 García, 91.
110 Amstutz, *Just Immigration*, 30.
111 García, *Refugee Challenge*, 120.
112 García, 127.

an individual was deemed a possible terrorist (a determination that did not require a trial). In that case, detention could be indefinite.[113] Even policies meant for good, such as an Obama-era policy requiring expedited hearings for detained immigrant minors, can backfire. In this instance, the quick timetable may not be enough time for a minor to find a pro bono lawyer, and few can afford to pay for one.[114]

Without the opportunities to have legal representation, to hear one's legal rights under US law, to have adequate time to build a defensive case for asylum, or to even appear before a court, opportunities regularly denied under various US laws and policies, it is incredibly difficult to establish one's refugee status, even in the most clear-cut of cases. It is not necessary to think that deportation is never an acceptable option (even the 1951 Refugee Convention allows for incarceration or deportation of war criminals and terrorists, for example) to see the problem here. As long as our international refugee system requires asylees to cross a border without permission to seek asylum, any legal system that denies due process to undocumented immigrants denies the rights of that portion of the undocumented who are refugees.

I have focused in this section on US instances of the denial of due process, but I do not wish to give the impression that this is a uniquely American phenomenon. Denial of due process for refugees is common across the globe. If we expand our scope slightly to include other North American countries, we see similar problems. María Christina García succinctly summarizes the situation in Mexico: "Article 33 of the Mexican Constitution

---

113 Micheline R. Ishay, *The History of Human Rights: From Ancient Times to the Globalization Era* (Berkeley: University of California Press, 2008), 280; Anna Sampaio, *Terrorizing Latina/o Immigrants: Race, Gender, and Immigration Politics in the Age of Security* (Philadelphia: Temple University Press, 2015), 70–71.
114 Dakin-Grimm, *Dignity and Justice*, 11.

allowed for the immediate expulsion of a foreigner without due process."[115] Luke and Mark Glanville recount the experiences of a Canadian community home for refugees known as Kinbrave: "Staff have come to realize that while a refugee's future will be decided at their refugee claim hearings, most claimants don't know in advance the most basic things about their hearings: where to go, what to expect, who is going to be there, or how the process will unfold."[116] A refugee without basic knowledge of the awaiting legal proceedings cannot reasonably be expected to prove their refugee status in court. It is sadly the case that when asylees finally get their day in court (and far too many are deported without this chance), they often arrive before a judge without the knowledge, evidence, representation, or financial means necessary to have any reasonable odds of proving their refugee status and securing their safety and right to employment and participation in goods like public education or political representation.

Refugees and the Intentional Denial of Justice

Thus far, I have treated the problems of delay, the militarization of border control, and the denial of due process as isolated phenomena, but they interlink and overlap to create an impossible situation for many refugees. Consider, for example, how the story of a refugee named Jospin illustrates the connections between these systems of injustice. Jospin had been unlawfully arrested, threatened, and beaten by police in Cameroon for being among the Anglophone minority, events that would surely qualify him for

---

115 García, *Seeking Refuge*, 67.
116 Glanville and Glanville, *Refuge Reimagined*, 114.

protection under the 1951 Refugee Convention. As discussed in chapter 2, past victimization by the state qualifies as "well-founded fear of persecution," and he further meets the necessary criteria because his persecution was due to inclusion in a particular social group (the English-speaking minority) and because he left his homeland being unable to seek protection from it. Fleeing Cameroon at age sixteen, Jospin tried to secure bus tickets to Libya but was denied because he lacked a passport, forcing him to turn to a series of smugglers to attempt to cross the militarized European border. Eventually, he was imprisoned and enslaved by these same smugglers. He finally managed to escape Libya and flee west but was captured crossing the border into Morocco, where he was beaten by police and threatened with worse if he returned.[117] Lacking other options, he crossed the Moroccan border again, successfully this time, eventually arriving at Melilla, a Spanish-owned city in Morocco and the only EU territory to have a land border with northern Africa. Melilla has a defensive network to deter immigrants, including three large fences of up to twenty feet tall. Illustrating the arbitrary nature of the logic behind militarizing border control, Reece Jones summarizes the situation: "If migrants make it over all three fences and set foot into the European Union, Spain is obligated to hear their asylum requests and provide them shelter. However, if they only make it over the first or second fence, they have not yet set foot in the European Union and can be returned to Morocco."[118] Jospin failed to cross the fences successfully several times and was beaten by police on multiple occasions. When he eventually made it into Melilla, he was knocked unconscious

---

117 Vella, *Dying to Live*, 81–86.
118 Jones, *Violent Borders*, 14.

by police and arrested.[119] Now he could have his chance to plead for asylum in court, yet the court attempted to deny due process. In his own words, "I had no time to explain. They just tell you what you did. All that my lawyer told me was that I had committed a crime. He didn't ask me what happened."[120] He was slated to be deported after a first hearing but finally was able to request asylum. Then came the delay, as he was left waiting for several years to hear whether he would receive asylum and be able to enter Europe to seek employment.[121] The militarization of border patrol, denial of due process, and delay converge to leave refugees like Jospin little chance of finding protection while greatly exacerbating his suffering.

After seeing the modern system of militarizing the border patrol, denial of due process, and delay, I am convinced that Jesus, Mary, and Joseph would have been less likely to face violence if they sought protection among the Jewish community in ancient Egypt than in modern Europe or the United States. After all, the Old Testament made provision in numerous places for the just treatment of foreigners with the law insisting on due process for migrants (Lev 19:33–34; Deut 1:16). Proverbs regularly addressed similar subjects, insisting that there should be no partiality in judgment (Prov 24:23b) and that the weights used for measurement when buying and selling should be honest (Prov 11:1; 16:11; 20:10; 20:23). One might rightly (in my opinion) extrapolate the principle of honest measurement in economic contexts and apply it in a legal context too: "Acquitting the guilty and condemning the just—both are detestable to the Lord" (Prov 17:15). Of course, Egyptian Jews might not have

---

119 Vella, *Dying to Live*, 86–87.
120 Vella, 87.
121 At the time of Vella's writing, the outcome of Jospin's asylum petition was unknown.

heeded the commandments, but even so, there was no substantive military apparatus used to prevent first-century travel from Judaea to Egypt. In contrast, much of the modern refugee regime is predicated upon forcefully preventing asylees from entering a potential host country and denying due process to those that do. If the holy family was seeking protection from Herod through the refugee system today, it would be unlikely they would ever receive it, either waiting in a camp or urban area for years on end in hopes of resettlement, facing violence that prevented them from seeing asylum as provided for in the law, or else choosing to live as undocumented rather than navigate the system. The next chapter will further explore why the European Union and United States repel refugees and asylees by analyzing the common (yet inaccurate) worries that immigrants are harmful to the economy and pose a security threat.

5

Unfounded Fears

As Jesus, Mary, and Joseph entered Egypt in the first century, there is a reasonable chance that they would have encountered discrimination or prejudice. The Torah recounts some animosity between Egyptians and the people of Israel at the time of Jacob's family's entrance into Egypt under Joseph's guidance: the Egyptians are said to not eat with Hebrews, for that is "abhorrent to them" (Gen 43:32). The same abhorrence is expressed toward Israelite shepherds (Gen 46:34) and, in the later time of Moses, toward the sacrifices Israel made to God (Exod 8:22). Though some Christians are aware of these texts in the Old Testament, few are likely aware that Egypt can be considered "the hothouse of the growth later labeled anti-Semitism," according to Peter

Schäfer.[1] By the time of the first century, several texts written in Egypt had renarrated the Jewish exodus account to claim that Jews were evil and diseased and so had been expelled from Egypt due to their causing plagues.[2] This narrative evolved to include accusations that Jews hated other peoples, destroyed their temples, and were afraid of foreigners.[3] Sometimes, the allegations against Egyptian Jews were even more atrocious, as, for example, when Apion, a hellenized Egyptian writer, accused Jews of kidnapping Greek foreigners, fattening them up for a year, then murdering and cannibalizing them.[4] Though our textual evidence is somewhat limited, it is clear that ugly anti-Semitism was present in Egypt and awaiting the holy family.

The prejudice of Egyptians against Jews was not limited to hateful stereotypes but was manifest at times in violence and injustice. For example, archaeologists have uncovered an ancient written petition by Helenos, an Alexandrian Jew, to the Roman prefect because he was being asked to pay taxes too high for an Alexandrian citizen (citizens had reduced taxes compared to noncitizen residents). Helenos had labeled himself an Alexandrian on the petition, but a scribe crossed this out and called him a Jew from Alexandria, thereby denying his claim to citizenship.[5] This scribal change suggests that Hellenistic Alexandrians might not have accepted Jews as citizens and that there were considerable financial and legal ramifications of this denial. In the year 38 CE, Hellenistic residents of Alexandria attempted to

---

1 Peter Schäfer, *Judeophobia: Attitudes toward the Jews in the Ancient World* (Cambridge, MA: Harvard University Press, 1997), 169.
2 Sandra Gambetti, *The Alexandrian Riots of 38 C.E. and the Persecution of the Jews: A Historical Reconstruction* (Leiden: Brill, 2009), 196–97.
3 Schäfer, *Judeophobia*, 163–69.
4 Miriam Pucci Ben Zeev, "Jews among Greeks and Romans," in Collins and Harlow, *Early Judaism*, 338. Apion wrote during the first half of the first century.
5 Ben Zeev, 338.

force Jews to put images of the emperor Gaius in their synagogues. When synagogue leaders refused, many houses of worship were destroyed. In response to the riot, the governor Flaccus stripped Jews in Alexandria of their status as residents and declared them foreigners, which meant they lost all right to appeal to Roman courts, being denied due process in a manner similar to refugees described in the previous chapter of this book.[6] Alexandrian Jews were stereotyped, excluded from certain civic rights, and subjected to periodic violence. Several weeks after fleeing Herod, Jesus's family would have entered this tense environment seeking shelter.

Jesus, Mary, and Joseph are not alone in facing hostility and resistance from a potential host country. In fact, one reason why refugees face such extreme militarized borders or wait indefinitely for resettlement is that the citizens of many potential host nations see refugees as a threat to national security or to the national economy. In both cases, the concern is overblown, and neither national security nor the economy justifies the neglect and hostility that many refugees face. To make that case, I now turn to consider the evidence of the impact of refugees on national security and the economy.

Refugees and National Security

One of the main concerns raised about immigrants in general and refugees in particular is that they pose a security threat to citizens in the European Union or the United States. Concerns are raised about crime and terrorism. For example, a 2017 survey found that "44 percent of Americans believe that illegal

---

6 Gambetti, *Alexandrian Riots of 38 C.E.*, 171–76.

immigration increased the level of serious crime in the United States."[7] Many think in the way that Matt C. Pinsker, former US special prosecutor, does when he writes, "People who enter our country illegally have broken the law; many of them will not respect the law once they are here."[8] This mindset ignores the fact that the international refugee regime expects and legally permits asylees and refugees to make undocumented border crossings. It also ignores the data about immigration and crime.[9]

Immigrants, Refugees, and Crime Rates

Despite concerns about refugees and immigrants causing crime, generally, studies find that immigrants and refugees are no more likely to commit crimes than native-born citizens, and in some contexts, they are less likely, though there is some variation from country to country based partly on various political, legal, social,

---

7 Matthew Soerens and Jenny Yang, *Welcoming the Stranger: Justice, Compassion, and Truth in the Immigration Debate*, rev. ed. (Downers Grove, IL: InterVarsity Books, 2018), 115.

8 Matt C. Pinsker, *Crisis on the Border: An Eyewitness Account of Illegal Aliens, Violent Crime, and Cartels* (Washington, DC: Regnery, 2020), 109.

9 Pinsker does not consider any statistical studies of immigration and crime in his chapter (appendixes include a few US Immigration and Customs Enforcement and Federal Bureau of Prisons reports from 2018 without any analysis) but does provide a tally of the illegal immigrants that appeared in court where he had access to their files, finding that one-third of them had previously been convicted of a criminal offense (110–12). US Customs and Border Protection keeps a record of all apprehensions and expulsions of undocumented immigrants or deportable immigrants as well as records of how many of these encounters were with individuals with prior criminal convictions. The national rates are that 11,623 of 404,142 encounters in FY2018 were with individuals who had a prior criminal conviction. In other words, where Pinsker says, "one in three illegal immigrants has been convicted of a crime," Border Patrol data say that 2.87 percent of them have. See "CBP Enforcement Statistics Fiscal Year 2021," US Customs and Border Protection, accessed August 16, 2021, https://www.cbp.gov/newsroom/stats/cbp-enforcement-statistics.

cultural, and economic factors.[10] When we consider the immigration process, this makes sense. When facing resettlement, after an initial screening by the United Nations High Commissioner for Refugees, refugees seeking to enter the United States are vetted by the Department of State, Homeland Security, the Department of Defense, the FBI, and the National Counterterrorism Center. This process involves checking crime databases with fingerprints and other biometric traces, so we should expect lower crime rates as those with a criminal history are excluded.[11] Furthermore, many asylees and refugees are fleeing precisely because they have refused to participate in violence or criminal activity in their homelands. Consider the example of Gilberto, a young Guatemalan who converted to Evangelicalism and began a Bible study ministry teaching children to "stand up for Jesus" and avoid gang life. When the Los Angeles–originating MS-13 gang, which is now an international force in Latin America, targeted Gilberto because of his faith, began to threaten to murder him if he did not sell drugs, beat him, and held him at gunpoint, Gilberto fled to the United States, knowing Guatemalan police rarely stand up to the stronger, more heavily armed MS-13.[12] If individuals like Gilberto had the strength to resist crime when their lives are being threatened, we can expect they will repeat the same decision in their host countries where social pressures

---

10 For example, where there are larger economic disparities between citizens and immigrants, crime rates may be higher for immigrants, since poverty is a predicting factor for crime rates. Similarly, when criminal background checks of immigrants are not possible, it may be harder to screen for criminal migrants. To my knowledge, a series of studies in Sweden in the 1980s and 1990s are the clearest example of a situation where immigrants tend to commit more crimes than native-born citizens, though data available at the time made it difficult to determine the factors behind these disparities. See Peter L. Martens, "Immigrants, Crime, and Criminal Justice in Sweden," *Crime and Justice* 21 (1997): 183–255. Generally, studies find the opposite connection, particularly in the United States.

11 For more on the process, see Bauman, Soerens, and Smeir, *Seeking Refuge*, 77.

12 Dakin-Grimm, *Dignity and Justice*, 4–8.

are likely to be less formidable. Looking more broadly at immigrants in general, the possibility of being deported for committing a crime serves as a deterrent to crime, so we can expect a further reduction in crime rates. This is especially true of undocumented immigrants who will want to avoid any interaction with law enforcement.[13] We expect immigrants and refugees to be less of a risk for crime than native-born citizens not because they are less likely to sin than citizens[14] but because those prone to the particular sins of violent and property crimes are apparently less likely to enter a country through an immigration process, including that for refugees and asylees.

Because much criminal data does not include information about whether the perpetrator was a refugee, most of our analysis will have to focus more broadly on immigrants. Perhaps the easiest way to consider the criminal effects of immigration is to study crime rates and immigration, which rarely correlate immigration with an increase in crime. Here, we might consider the national crime rates for nations that have accepted large numbers of refugees. As Serena Parekh notes, despite high levels of refugee admissions in European countries like Germany and Italy, crime is falling. In Germany, crime is at its lowest level in thirty years, and in Italy, crime fell by 25 percent between 2007 and 2016.[15] Such general claims are not the most robust way to examine crime rates, but more precise statistical analyses consistently find that immigrants are not any more prone to crime than native-born

---

13 Anne Morrison Piehl, "Testimony of Anne Morrison Piehl, Ph.D., Department of Economics and Program in Criminal Justice, Rutgers, the State University of New Jersey," in *Comprehensive Immigration Reform: Impact of Immigration on States and Localities. Hearing before the Subcommittee on Immigration, Citizenship, Refugees, Border Security, and International Law of the Committee on the Judiciary, House of Representatives, One Hundred Tenth Congress* (Washington, DC: US GPO, 2007), 82.

14 As Paul makes clear in Rom 3, all sin.

15 Parekh, *No Refuge*, xvi.

citizens and, in some situations, are less likely to commit a crime than citizens. Kristin Butcher and Anne Morrison Piehl used survey data from 2000 and 2005 to calculate the percentage of immigrants in twenty-nine major Californian cities, comparing this percentage with violent crime and property crime rates. They found no statistically significant correlation between immigration rates and property crime rates, but there was a statistically significant correlation between increased immigration rates and a decline in violent crimes.[16] Similar results have been found in other studies.[17] Of course, correlation does not mean causation, but the findings are helpful in dissuading fears of immigrant crime nonetheless. Other studies find no correlation between immigration and crime—a growing immigrant population apparently neither raises nor lowers crime rates. Studying 1,252 locations in 2000 and 2005–7, of which 573 were identified as the targets of larger groups of incoming immigrants, Vincent Ferraro used a violent crime index (tabulating murder, robbery, and assault) and a nonviolent crime index (tabulating burglary, larceny, and motor vehicle theft) to see whether those cities with growing immigrant populations were more prone to crime. He analyzed the data through various models that controlled for different factors like poverty, age, and ethnicity, finding that "contrary to the expectation of a significant negative effect within the full sample of places, change in immigration exerted no significant effect on change in crime, whether violent,

---

16 Kristin F. Butcher, Anne Morrison Piehl, and Jay Liao, *Crime, Corrections, and California: What Does Immigration Have to Do with It?* California Counts: Population Trends and Profiles, vol. 9, no. 3 (February 2008), 17–18.

17 See John M. MacDonald, John R. Hipp, and Charlotte Gill, "The Effects of Immigrant Concentration on Changes in Neighborhood Crime Rates," *Journal of Quantitative Criminology* 29, no. 2 (June 2013): 191–215.

property, or total crime."[18] On the other hand, an increase in the ratio of adults to children (likely suggesting a rise in single young adults) and an increase in "disadvantage" were both clear predictors of an increase in crime.[19] Such data suggest that fears about immigrants causing crime are mistaken.[20]

What about refugees and asylees more specifically? Here, we have fewer studies to go by, but evidence still suggests that refugees and asylees do not increase crime rates. Last chapter, we considered the situation of Haitians and Cubans with their disparate treatment under US deterrence policies and the denial of due process during the 1970s through the 2000s. During the same period, some raised concerns about crime brought to the United States by both groups, and fears about Cuban criminality were even depicted in cinema, most notably in the Golden Globe nominee *Scarface*.[21] Ramiro Martinez and Matthew Lee analyzed crimes in Miami, when the Miami police department began to indicate whether perpetrators and suspects of crimes were Mariel Cuban, Haitian, or Jamaican in addition to the usual white, Black, and Latino designations. Given the high percentage of refugees, asylum seekers, and nonconvention refugees who might seek entry without permission among Haitians and Cubans, crime rates in each can give an estimate of the crime

---

18 Vincent Ferraro, *Immigrants and Crime in the New Destinations* (El Paso, TX: LFB Scholarly, 2014), 140.

19 Ferraro, 141.

20 Here are several further studies to consider: I. A. Hourwich, "Immigration and Crime," *American Journal of Sociology* 17, no. 4 (January 1912): 478–90; Richard Stansfield et al., "Assessing the Effects of Recent Immigration on Serious Property Crime in Austin, Texas," *Sociological Perspectives* 56, no. 4 (Winter 2013): 647–72; and Matthew T. Lee, Ramiro Martinez Jr., and Richard Rosenfeld, "Does Immigration Increase Homicide? Negative Evidence from Three Border Cities," *Sociological Quarterly* 42, no. 4 (Autumn 2001): 559–80.

21 For a discussion of fears of Mariel refugees at the time, see Jillian Marie Jacklin, "The Cuban Criminal: Media Reporting and the Production of a Popular Image," *International Journal of Cuban Studies* 11, no. 1 (Summer 2019): 61–83.

threat posed by these refugee groups. From 1980 to 1984, the city homicide rate was 67.9 homicides per 100,000 people. Mariels and Haitians were at 55.5 and 26.4 per 100,000, respectively. The Jamaican rate (another immigrant group the study considered) at this time was higher, at 102.2 per 100,000, one of the rare instances in the literature I have surveyed of higher immigrant crime rates. By 1990, however, the city rate had dropped to 49.9 per 100,000 while immigrant rates dropped even lower with Mariel, Haitian, and Jamaican rates at 10.5, 12.8, and 15.9 per 100,000, respectively.[22] In some circumstances, asylees do run contrary to the trend of immigrants as a whole when it comes to property crime rates. When large populations of asylees (or undocumented immigrants, for that matter) enter a country but are not permitted to work, there can be an associated increase in property crimes like theft and burglary.[23] This is not surprising, as a lack of economic opportunities is a predictor of criminal activity. Fortunately, studies have also found that access to labor markets corrects this rise in property crime, dropping asylees and undocumented immigrants to crime rates comparable to native-born citizens.[24]

---

22 Ramiro Martinez Jr. and Matthew T. Lee, "Comparing the Context of Immigrant Homicides in Miami: Haitians, Jamaicans, and Mariels," *International Migration Review* 34, no. 3 (Autumn 2000): 794–812.

23 Bell, Fasani, and Machen found no rise in violent crime rates at the time of two "large immigrant waves" to the United Kingdom. The first wave was correlated with a "modest but significant rise in property crimes," while the second correlated with a negligible decline in property crimes. Notably, the first wave of asylees were often legally prohibited from employment. Brian Bell, Francesco Fasani, and Stephen Machin, "Crime and Immigration: Evidence from Large Immigrant Waves," *Review of Economics and Statistics* 95, no. 4 (October 2013): 1278–90.

24 For example, when the United States passed the 1986 Immigration Reform and Control Act (IRCA), legalizing most undocumented immigrants, there was a decline in property crimes of 3 to 5 percent associated with the change. Scott R. Baker, "Effects of Immigrant Legalization on Crime," *American Economic Review* 105, no. 5 (May 2015): 210–13. Similar results have been found in Italy when undocumented Romanians and Bulgarians were given a path to legal residence. Giovanni Mastrobuoni and Paolo Pinotti, "Legal Status and the Criminal Activity of Immigrants," *American Economic Journal: Applied Economics* 7, no. 2 (April 2015): 175–206.

Alternative Methods of Measuring Immigration and Crime

While the study of immigration and crime rates can be helpful, it is not a foolproof approach to considering immigration and crime. It may be that undocumented immigrants are less likely to report crimes, for example, and therefore that immigrant crime rates are skewed. On the other hand, inaccurate estimates of the number of undocumented immigrants in a community may skew crime rates in either direction by misunderstanding the actual total population relative to the number of crimes, placing immigrant communities in a more positive light or more negative light than is deserved. For this reason, we would do well to consider other approaches to exploring the impact of immigration on crime that do not rely on crime rates within a fixed population. In one particularly telling study, Luca Nunziata analyzed data from the European Social Survey that covered sixteen Western European destination countries for immigrants.[25] Every two years, this survey asks several questions of Europeans, including whether they have been the victim of a crime and the extent to which they fear for their safety in their community. Nunziata found that crimes did not increase with a growth in immigration, but the fear of crime tellingly did.[26] Such victimization studies are not subject to distortion by misestimating the total population size due to miscounting undocumented immigrants. The key point, though, is this: despite a lack of any evidence that immigration raises crime rates, many Europeans wrongly fear crime more as immigrants arrive in their communities.

---

25 Countries include Austria, Belgium, Switzerland, Germany, Denmark, Spain, Finland, France, Greece, Ireland, Luxembourg, Netherlands, Norway, Portugal, Sweden, and the United Kingdom.

26 Luca Nunziata, "Immigration and Crime: Evidence from Victimization Data," *Journal of Population Economics* 28, no. 3 (July 2015): 723.

We might also consider whether stricter immigration enforcement has any effect on reducing crime. If undocumented immigrants are disproportionately committing crimes, then policies designed to remove such immigrants should decrease crime. Thomas Miles and Adam Cox consider whether crime rates decrease in Secure Communities that allow law enforcement to check for immigration status and deport those who are undocumented. However, no correlation was found between strict immigration enforcement and a reduction in crime.[27] A study by the Cato Institute found similar results. In North Carolina, the 287(g) program allowed local law enforcement to enforce federal immigration law, resulting in higher rates of deportation of undocumented immigrants. The Cato Institute study found no correlation between the rollout of this program in various counties and a decline in crime. However, this program did result in more assaults on police officers as undocumented immigrants went to extreme measures to remain in the country when being apprehended.[28] Generally, though, there is no evidence that stricter immigration enforcement reduces crime.

Incarceration Rates among Immigrants

Though there is little evidence of immigrants increasing crime rates, this fear commonly drives immigration policy. I suspect this is due to a range of causes, from media depictions to the rhetoric of politicians, from social psychology to nativism and

---

27 Thomas J. Miles and Adam B. Cox, "Does Immigration Enforcement Reduce Crime? Evidence from Secure Communities," *Journal of Law & Economics* 57, no. 4 (November 2014): 937–73.

28 Andrew Forrester and Alex Nowrasteh, *Do Immigration Enforcement Programs Reduce Crime? Evidence from the 287(g) Program in North Carolina* (Washington, DC: Cato Institute, 2018).

racial bigotry, each cause influencing different sectors of society. However, one factor directly related to our discussion of immigration and crime is incarceration rates. In the 1980s and '90s in the United States, for example, a relatively large fraction of the prison population consisted of immigrant men. This might suggest that higher percentages of immigrants are committing crimes. However, this phenomenon can be misleading for several reasons.[29] First, higher percentages of immigrants are young males, and two major predictors of crime are being male and being between the ages of fifteen and thirty-four.[30] One study in California found that among comparable age groups, "U.S.-born men ages 18–40 have institutionalization rates that are 10 times higher than those of foreign-born men in the same age group (4.2% vs. 0.42%)."[31] Second, undocumented immigrants are far less likely to be given bail, which can result in an inability to generate resources to mount a court defense, increasing the likelihood of conviction. Third, immigrants are more likely to be incarcerated when convicted of drug crimes than citizens, even though they are less likely to have a criminal history.[32] The imbalance in sentencing suggests that justice is not blind to one's immigration status. These factors together lead Hagan and Palloni to rightly conclude that "An overreliance on prison statistics is a problematic basis for developing our understanding of immigration and crime."[33] The broader evidence suggests that

---

29 Studies like Zehnder, *Bible and Immigration*, which focus almost exclusively on incarceration rates, are fatally flawed because they do not consider such factors.

30 John Hagan and Alberto Palloni, "Immigration and Crime in the United States," in *The Immigration Debate: Studies on the Economic, Demographic, and Fiscal Effects of Immigration*, ed. James P. Smith and Barry Edmonston (Washington, DC: National Academy Press, 1998), 374–75.

31 Butcher, Piehl, and Liao, *Crime, Corrections, and California*, 10.

32 Hagan and Palloni, "Immigration and Crime," 376.

33 Hagan and Palloni, 380.

immigrants are no more likely to commit crimes than citizens and often are less likely to do so.

Refugees and Terrorism

Immigrants in general and refugees in particular are sometimes viewed as a terrorist threat. An instructive example of this fear is found in Darrell Ankarlo, a broadcaster who explores his worries about terrorism in his book *Another Man's Sombrero*. Ankarlo begins his discussion by noting the large number of arrested undocumented immigrants who are released from detention into the United States during their trial process. (Presumably, many would be in the process of making a defensive asylum case.) Ankarlo asks, "Is anyone else concerned that 45,000 potential terrorists are loose on U.S. soil?"[34] Referencing several intelligence reports that warn of the risk of terrorist attacks at the southern border and sharing a transcript of a Saudi Arabian man who has called Ankarlo's radio show claiming to know that he knew terrorists were trying to sneak across the southern border, Ankarlo insists that "our less-than-perfect bureaucratic system seems to beg for another September 11 attack."[35] This is not a uniquely American concern. In a survey of ten European nations, a majority of respondents in eight of the nations believed that resettling refugees increases the risk of domestic terrorism.[36] Is this a reasonable concern?

---

34 Darrell Ankarlo, *Another Man's Sombrero: A Conservative Broadcaster's Undercover Journey across the Mexican Border* (Nashville: Thomas Nelson, 2008), 234.
35 Ankarlo, 237.
36 Richard Wike, Bruce Stokes, and Katie Simmons, "Europeans Fear Wave of Refugees Will Mean More Terrorism, Fewer Jobs: Sharp Ideological Divides across EU on Views about Minorities, Diversity, and National Identity," Pew Research Center, July 11, 2016, 30.

To evaluate how serious the threat of terrorism is, it is necessary to move beyond rumors and semianonymous radio talk show callers to consider the data. One helpful place to start is with American antiterrorism operations against undocumented immigrants. After the 9/11 terrorist attacks in the United States, "Operation Tarmac," a joint effort spearheaded by the newly created Department of Homeland Security and other agencies, closely examined employment records at airports and facilities near airports such as hotels and restaurants. The operation examined over three-quarters of a million records to identify several thousand undocumented workers, mostly Latinx immigrants. US attorneys described the effort as "a highly effective weapon in the domestic war on terrorism," but officials now admit not a single individual identified through the operation had a tie with any terrorist group.[37] Despite this, government officials describe the operation as necessary to protect against terrorism. Though undocumented immigrants are often scapegoated as security threats, when Anna Sampaio surveyed all US immigration raids from 2001 to 2008, she found that no evidence of terrorist activity was found, nor were any terrorists arrested.[38] Sampaio explains, "The operations targeted 'persons of unknown origin'—terminology that became synonymous with undocumented Latina/o immigrants."[39] Such inaccurate depictions are one aspect of the nativism and racial stereotyping that many migrants face in their new countries.

It makes little sense for terrorists to use the refugee system to try to enter a country due to low resettlement rates, extensive

---

37 Sampaio, *Terrorizing Latina/o Immigrants*, 6.
38 Sampaio, 85.
39 Sampaio, 88. For example, Sampaio notes one raid on the Houston airport in the name of national security, which resulted in the arrest of 143 individuals, all Latina/o, none terrorists.

background checks, and the protracted nature of the procedure. The asylum procedure is equally complicated, making it an unlikely venue for terrorists. It would make far more sense for terrorists to use less protected travel options, such as the seventy million tourist visas granted to the United States each year.[40] For this reason among others, there have been very few terrorist attacks based on the asylum or refugee systems. The 1993 World Trade Center bombing in New York included one perpetrator who had entered the country with a forged passport and, when caught, claimed asylum.[41] The time between 1993 and 2003 included 212 suspected and convicted terrorists; the largest category had tourist visas, but 16 percent had applied for asylum.[42] The 9/11 terrorist attacks on the World Trade Center, the Pentagon, and Flight 93 involved individuals who were all present in the country through tourist or student visas. Sadly, US intelligence and law enforcement agencies knew many of these terrorists were a threat but, prior to the Homeland Security Act, did not share this information with the Immigration and Naturalization Service.[43]

In another study, a researcher at the Cato Institute analyzed the immigration status of all terrorist foreigners in the United States since 1975 compared with normal immigration rates and found that one terrorist entered as a refugee for every 135,648 refugees total, and one terrorist was granted asylum for every 66,561 individuals granted asylum. Only three of twenty-five refugee terrorists succeeded in their plans, killing two in the 1970s before the 1980 Refugee Act initiated stricter security

40 Bauman, Soerens, and Smeir, *Seeking Refuge*, 78.
41 García, *Refugee Challenge*, 114–17.
42 García, 125.
43 García, 124–25.

screening for refugees. Nine Americans were killed by asylee terrorists, though three of these deaths came from children admitted as asylees who were radicalized while in the United States.[44] Since 1975, more Americans have died on average each year from wolf or bear attacks than the average deaths from acts of terrorism committed by refugees or asylees. Considerably more have died of lightning strikes.[45] Findings are similar in Europe, where terrorists tend to be citizens in an EU nation rather than refugees or asylees.[46] In fact, some have argued that leaving refugees in camps for decades is a greater terrorist threat, as disillusioned refugees could be radicalized by terrorist recruiters, though there is limited evidence such recruitment is currently underway.[47]

I should note that article 1F of the 1951 Refugee Convention excludes anyone who has committed war crimes or acts contrary to the purposes of the United Nations from protection under the convention. Guy Goodwin-Gil summarizes, "From the beginning, therefore, the 1951 Convention has contained clauses sufficient to ensure that the serious criminal and the terrorist do not benefit from international protection."[48] It is certainly important to exclude war criminals, terrorists, and violators of human rights from refugee resettlement and asylum, yet the widespread sense that terrorism is a large threat to the refugee system is simply mistaken.

44 Alex Nowrasteh, *Terrorists by Immigration Status and Nationality: A Risk Analysis, 1975–2017* (Washington, DC: Cato Institute, 2019), 23–24.
45 Rates taken from Jennifer Rebecca Kelly et al., "Large Carnivore Attacks on Humans: The State of Knowledge," *Human Ecology Review* 25, no. 2 (2019): 15–34.
46 See Manni Crone, Maja Felicia Falkentoft, and Teemu Tammikko, *Europe's Refugee Crisis and the Threat of Terrorism: An Extraordinary Threat?* Danish Institute for International Studies Report (Copenhagen, Denmark: January 1, 2017).
47 Daniel Milton, Megan Spencer, and Michael Findley, "Radicalism of the Hopeless: Refugee Flows and Transnational Terrorism," *International Interactions: Empirical and Theoretical Research in International Relations* 39, no. 5 (2013): 621–45.
48 Goodwin-Gill, "International Law," 39.

Refugees and asylees generally do not pose a security threat. Terrorist acts by refugees and asylees are exceedingly rare and have become even more so with recent, more expansive capabilities of the background check of those seeking protection. Typically, refugees and asylees commit crimes at rates equal to or lower than native-born citizens. One notable exception is when refugees and asylees are prevented from working, at which point more tend to participate in property crimes as a source of revenue. Governments can easily eliminate such crimes by offering paths to employment. However, many citizens of the United States and EU member states raise economic concerns about welcoming refugees into the labor force, so we must now turn to these concerns.

Economic Concerns

The economic impact of immigrants is often a factor in leading citizens of various nations to be hesitant or hostile to accepting refugees. Several studies demonstrate this point. For example, according to one survey, the number of Americans who believe immigrants come primarily for welfare programs, seeking a handout, is higher than the number who believe that immigrants come primarily for jobs.[49] After the end of World War II, numerous polls found that Americans were, on the majority, opposed to resettling refugees for fear that it would increase unemployment.[50] In times of recession, this fear can be particularly acute. Tensions grew in Italy roughly a decade ago until several acts of racism and mass violence were carried out, first when several

---

49 Marisa Abrajano and Zoltan L. Hajnal, *White Backlash: Immigration, Race, and American Politics* (Princeton, NJ: Princeton University Press, 2015), 35.

50 Zolberg, *Nation by Design*, 304–5.

hundred Italians attacked a Roma camp with firebombs and then when several Bangladeshi vendors' carts were attacked.[51] Are such concerns about the economic harm brought about by immigrants in general, and refugees in particular, valid? It turns out, the answer to the question depends to a degree on what you measure and how you measure it, but as a whole, the economic impact of refugees seems to be far less harmful than often feared.

My analysis will especially, though not exclusively, focus on the economic impact of undocumented immigrants and of refugees in several areas of the economy. I choose to focus on undocumented immigrants because, as we have seen, many refugees must first cross a country's borders without its legal permission to seek asylum. Others tired of waiting in refugee camps will decide to leave camps to enter host countries to live in urban areas without permission, while still others fleeing violence who do not meet the technical definition of a refugee will feel they have no choice but to cross a border without documents or to overstay the expiration of a short-term visa. Often, the boundary between asylees, refugees, and undocumented immigrants can be quite blurred, especially for individuals fleeing to urban settings who might avoid formal legal processes of recognition.[52] Of course, many refugees who are resettled through the United Nations will fall under the category of legal immigrants, so I will discuss data concerning legal immigration as well. However, because undocumented immigrants tend to be more controversial, considering such data may be more beneficial. Furthermore, because the economic impact of undocumented immigrants is typically politically contentious, there is more extensive literature

---

51 Jayati Ghosh, "Fear of Foreigners: Recession and Racism in Europe," *Race/Ethnicity: Multidisciplinary Global Contexts* 4, no. 2 (Winter 2011): 188.
52 See the discussion in Hamlin, "Ideology, International Law, and the INS," 334–35.

on the economic costs of undocumented immigrants than on the costs of refugees. In fact, many large data sets used in the analysis of the economic impact of immigrants do not include refugees as a distinct category, making full analysis more difficult. I turn now to consider different measures of the economic impact of refugees, offering a representative survey of evidence, if not an exhaustive one due to space constraints.

Gross Domestic Product and Refugees

Gross domestic product (GDP) refers to the sum of all economic transactions in an economy, including consumption, investment, government spending, and net exports. It is often treated as a basic measurement of the size and growth of an economy. A quick look at the recipient countries of the immense Syrian refugee migration shows that economic growth can continue with surprisingly high refugee levels. Serena Parekh summarizes, "In 2015, with 2.2 million refugees, Turkey's economy exploded by 3 percent; Lebanon, which took in 1.1 million refugees, saw economic growth of 2–3 percent; and Jordan, which hosts over 600,000 refugees, also had 3 percent economic growth that year."[53] Note that Lebanon only had a population of about 6.5 million at the time. Clearly, enormous arrivals of refugees do not guarantee that a nation will stop seeing economic growth. However, GDP is not necessarily the best measure of the economic impact of refugees because it does not tell us about the distribution of wealth in such countries, nor does it consider the potential economic strain on public services like education

---

53 Parekh, *No Refuge*, xvii.

and health care that the arrival of refugees may cause.[54] In countries with enormously high ratios of refugees to citizens, like Lebanon, we can expect a decline in per capita GDP.

The Fiscal Impact of Immigrants

Sometimes resistance to immigration is rooted in concerns about the drag immigrants will create on national, state, and local budgets. When we consider undocumented immigrants, the perceived problem is particularly acute given the expectation that they will draw on welfare programs and public services but not pay taxes.[55] This perception is likely overinflated. As early as the 1970s, David North and Marion Houstoun interviewed 850 undocumented immigrants in the United States and found that 77.3 percent reported paying social security, 73.2 percent had federal income tax withheld, but only 31.5 percent filed tax returns, meaning the majority could expect no tax refund.[56] When you factor in taxes like sales tax, which are unavoidably paid in most purchases, undocumented immigrants pay considerable amounts of taxes. Refugees who enter a country legally and have no reason to be paid under the table can be expected to pay social security, federal, and state taxes. There is undoubtedly some skimping on tax obligations among undocumented immigrants, some of whom would be asylum seekers or non-convention refugees not qualifying for official protection. However, based on North and Houstoun's surveys, we have reason to

---

54 In fact, this is a weakness of Parekh's argument, as she does not consider per capita GDP, which would have declined during the same period.

55 Many health care– and education-related public services prohibit questioning the immigration status of the recipient, and many undocumented immigrants do work for cash, being paid under the table.

56 David North and Marion Houstoun, *The Characteristics and Role of Illegal Aliens in the U.S. Labor Market: An Exploratory Study* (Washington, DC: Linton, 1976).

suspect that income tax evasion is not the norm. Despite this evidence, immigrants are depicted as a fiscal burden. In the 1990s, for example, California passed Proposition 187, which would deny undocumented immigrants access to social services, public education, and health care, though the bill was eventually struck down. When presented with evidence that immigrants actually underutilize state-funded health care programs, Harold Ezell, coauthor of Proposition 187, simply replied that the researcher had "obviously never been to any of the emergency rooms in Orange County to see who's using them—it's non-English-speaking young people with babies."[57] At times, data collected using sound scientific methodology can be rejected based on how a situation is perceived anecdotally, which is especially problematic when one's perceptions are shaped by nativism or racism.

Even if undocumented immigrants are paying taxes, might they still be a fiscal burden? This is a valid question, and our answer to it will depend on what data we draw on. Some American defenders of undocumented immigrants like to point to the net gains for social security and Medicare that come from such immigrants.[58] In 2013, the Office of the Chief Actuary of the Social Security Administration estimated that 3.1 million unauthorized immigrants paid taxes under false social security numbers. Assuming undocumented immigrants made up 80 percent of the average citizen/legal immigrant, this projects a $13 billion revenue for social security. The same report estimated

---

57 George J. Sánchez, "Face the Nation: Race, Immigration, and the Rise of Nativism in Late-Twentieth Century America," in Hirschman, Kasinitz, and Dewind, *Handbook of International Migration*, 378.
58 For example, Sarah Quezada, *Love Undocumented: Risking Trust in a Fearful World* (Harrisonburg, VA: Herald, 2018), 88.

only $1 billion paid out to undocumented immigrants.[59] Turning to consider legal immigrants, a study by Michael Clune of tax revenues in California found that in 1994, 27 percent of native households received social security, with roughly the same number receiving Medicare, but only 15.2 percent of immigrant households received social security, and only 16.2 percent received Medicare.[60] Such disparities may partly be due to the average age of immigrant households, as well as the fact that immigrant households tend to have more children, resulting in a younger population cross-generationally than in native-born households. This data shows that admitting refugees can be a savvy way to bolster social services for the elderly in nations with an aging population.[61]

On the other hand, larger numbers of children equate to higher educational expenses, which may place a larger burden on state budgets. At times, this has been a political issue. For example, in 1994, the governors of Florida, California, Arizona, Illinois, and New Jersey sued the federal government to ask for reimbursement of state expenses for undocumented immigrants, given that states bore the costs of education and emergency health services, but immigration was solely a federal responsibility that the federal government was, allegedly, negligent in fulfilling. For sake of efficiency, I will focus on the claims of California, the state in which undocumented immigrants had the largest fiscal impact. California is also an important state to consider because in 1992, 32.7 percent of asylees indicated California as

59 Stephen Goss et al., "Effects of Unauthorized Immigration on the Actuarial Status of the Social Security Trust Funds," Actuarial Note 151 (Baltimore, MD: Social Security Administration Office of the Chief Actuary, 2013).
60 Michael S. Clune, "The Fiscal Impacts of Immigrants: A California Case Study," in Smith and Edmonston, *Immigration Debate*, 140.
61 A point well made in Bauman, Soerens, and Smeir, *Seeking Refuge*, 68.

their intended state of residence in their asylum paperwork.[62] Pete Wilson, governor of California, estimated $3.2 billion spent per year on "services for illegal immigrants and their families in response to federal mandates."[63] In response, the Office of Management and Budget, within the executive office, commissioned a report from the Urban Institute on the costs of illegal immigration in comparison with tax revenues. This report estimated only $1.779 billion is spent annually on undocumented immigrants, with $732 million in tax revenue, resulting in a net loss of just over $1 billion a year.[64] Such studies suggest that undocumented immigrants, which would include some asylum seekers and some who flee but do not meet the technical definition of a refugee, can be a financial burden on state budgets, but the story is not quite so simple.

As the divergent estimates between the governor of California and the Urban Institute study requested by Congress reveal, analyses of the fiscal impact of undocumented immigrants are precisely that: *estimates*. Different estimates about the average household income of immigrants, decisions about whether to count educational costs of US-born citizen children of undocumented immigrants in studies,[65] and a lack of definitive counts

---

62 Clune, "Fiscal Impacts," 120.

63 *Increasing Costs of Illegal Immigration: Hearing before the Committee on Appropriations, United States Senate, One Hundred Third Congress, Section Session, Special Hearing* (Washington, DC: US GPO, 1994), 17, 20.

64 Rebecca L. Clark et al., *Fiscal Impacts of Undocumented Aliens: Selected Estimates for Seven States* (Washington, DC: Urban Institute, 1994), 50, 101, 129, 146.

65 As Lee and Miller note, counting US-born citizen children of undocumented immigrants can especially sway results because these children typically aren't factored in once they are adults and paying taxes, only when they are children incurring educational costs. Ronald D. Lee and Timothy W. Miller, "The Current Fiscal Impact of Immigrants and Their Descendants: Beyond the Immigrant Household," in Smith and Edmonston, *Immigration Debate*, 184.

of the population of undocumented immigrants[66] all can result in different numbers, though one survey of global studies of the fiscal impact of immigration found that estimates of the fiscal impact of immigrants tend to range from a net cost of 1 percent of GDP to a net gain of 1 percent of GDP.[67] I want to focus on three other reasons why state-level fiscal analysis is complicated: (1) economic analysis should consider the economic benefits across generations; (2) the policy choices of a state, especially its tax policies, can dramatically change the economic impact of the immigrant community; and (3) the fiscal impact of immigrants ought to be situated within the larger economic impact of immigrant communities.

Returning to California, we can see that the matter is more complicated once we consider multiple generations of immigrants. Michael Clune drew on various surveys and data sets in the 1990s to study the fiscal impact of immigrants in California.[68] Clune found that first-generation immigrants paid lower taxes (typically because they earned less), and they had more children, costing the state more for educational expenses.[69] By the third generation, however, descendants of immigrants were found to be a fiscal benefit at federal, state, and local levels, paying higher taxes on average than other native-born households.[70] Clune also notes that "the average household [native and

---

66 For example, a study of the fiscal impact of undocumented immigrants in San Diego found school districts unwilling to interview a representative sampling of students in Limited English Proficiency programs to identify their immigration status as a basis for estimating county-wide numbers. Instead, they simply asked forty administrators to estimate numbers and calculated costs based on these guesses. Richard A. Parker and Louis M. Rea, *Illegal Immigration in San Diego County: An Analysis of Costs and Revenues* (San Diego: Rea & Parker, 1993), 133–35.

67 Robert Hawthorn, "The Fiscal Impact of Immigration on the Advanced Economies," *Oxford Review of Economic Policy* 24, no. 3 (Autumn 2008): 560–80.

68 Clune does not restrict his analysis to undocumented immigrants.

69 Clune, "Fiscal Impacts," 149.

70 Clune, 160.

immigrant] is a net burden on all three levels of government, receiving $6,535 more in services than paid in taxes."[71] Given that the federal government consistently runs a deficit—and that state revenue also comes from corporate taxes, fees, and tourism—this should not be a surprise.

Ronald Lee and Timothy Miller consider the way that various analyses of undocumented immigrants can skew data. Looking at the national immigrant population in 1994, Lee and Miller count only immigrants and estimate $32.4 billion net tax revenue ($28.2 federal, $4.2 state and local). If we count immigrant households, including US-born citizen children up to age twenty, the estimate is a net loss of $13.3 billion ($16 billion gain at a federal level but a $29.3 billion loss at the state and local level). If we track citizen children through their adulthood, the estimate is $29.5 billion net revenue ($48.9 gain at a federal level but $19.3 loss at a state/local level).[72] Keep in mind that these studies are estimates, not exact accounting records. The divergent results reveal that who is considered in a study of the fiscal impact of immigrants matters immensely, and politicians, reporters, and even ethicists like me can be selective in which immigrants are counted to argue for divergent conclusions. A more expansive survey of studies suggests, however, that first-generation refugees, asylum seekers, and those who flee without meeting the legal definition of a refugee may be a fiscal drag on states like California. These results must be contextualized with the fact that on average, families of citizens also cause a fiscal loss in California, a state that relies on revenue from tourism to balance the budget. Plus, the deficit will diminish

---

71 Clune, 153.
72 Lee and Miller, "Immigrants and Their Descendants," 198.

across generations.[73] When we consider only one generation, we do not get the full picture, and even cross-generational studies can differ.

Of course, the cross-generational effect of immigration on the economy is further complicated in the case of refugees, many of whom hope to be repatriated to their country once periods of persecution have ended, much as the holy family returned to Judaea after the death of Herod (Matt 2:19–23). In some instances, refugees or asylees can be anticipated to remain in a host country, along with their descendants, for generations. In others, repatriation may be possible within a short time frame. Sometimes, refugee groups might repatriate only to need to flee again as a result of further political instability or regime changes.[74] All of these factors suggest that the economic impact of refugees will be difficult to fully predict, because the cross-generational benefit of immigration is uncertain.

A second factor that complexifies a fiscal analysis of the effects of immigration is the differences in policy at a state level. For example, one of the main sources of expense for a state when it comes to undocumented immigration is incarceration, but governments have the ability to decriminalize, selectively enforce, or rely on methods other than incarceration to reduce their expenses and increase net revenue from undocumented immigrants. No doubt, such topics are controversial, and this is not a book on the ethics of incarceration,[75] so let me point to another example:

---

73 One longitudinal study found that refugees increased their earnings (and thus their tax payments) more quickly than economic immigrants, probably largely due to support that allows for quicker accumulation of human capital and English proficiency. See Kalena E. Cortes, "Are Refugees Different from Economic Immigrants? Some Empirical Evidence on the Heterogeneity of Immigrant Groups in the United States," *Review of Economics and Statistics* 86, no. 2 (May 2004): 465–80.

74 For a helpful summary on repatriation, see "NGO Statement on Voluntary Repatriation (22–24 May 2002)," *Refugee Survey Quarterly* 22, nos. 2/3 (2003): 420–28.

75 I personally favor reduced criminalization of many immigration violations.

income tax. States like Texas that do not have an income tax tend to benefit from undocumented immigrants, since those lacking a social security number who receive cash payments are not avoiding any taxes. Instead, they pay full taxes through sales tax, property tax, and other fees. For example, Carole Strayhorn, the Republican comptroller of Texas, estimated that the 1.4 million undocumented immigrants in Texas in 2005 resulted in a net gain of $424.7 million in revenue.[76] This finding is consistent with a study from the University of Texas in 1984 that found between $122 and $179 million in positive revenue to the state from undocumented immigrants.[77] Apparently, the many asylum seekers and other undocumented immigrants who have crossed into Texas have been a financial benefit to that state's budget.[78] The fiscal impact of undocumented immigrants varies depending on the state in consideration based on various policies chosen by that state, including the state's tax structure. Notably, the increased criminalization of undocumented immigration discussed in chapter 4 can also greatly increase the costs of incarceration, one of the three largest areas of expense[79] associated with undocumented immigrants.

---

76 Carole Keeton Strayhorn, *Undocumented Immigrants in Texas: A Financial Analysis of the Impact to the State Budget and Economy*, Office of the Comptroller (Austin, TX: December 2006), 20.

77 Sidney Weintraub and Gilberto Cardenas, *The Use of Public Services by Undocumented Aliens in Texas: A Study of State Costs and Revenues*, Policy Research Report, no. 60 (Austin, TX: Lyndon B. Johnson School of Public Affairs, 1984).

78 Other studies have found similar results in other states. For example, one study in Nebraska estimated that immigrants paid $1,554 per capita in taxes while receiving only $1,445 per capita in benefits, a net profit to the state larger than that of native-born residents. Christopher Decker, Jerry Deichert, and Lourdes Gouveia, *Nebraska's Immigrant Population: Economic and Fiscal Impacts*, OLLAS Special Report No. 5 (Omaha, NE: Office of Latino/Latin American Studies [OLLAS], University of Nebraska at Omaha, 2008), 1.

79 The other areas are medical care (primarily through programs like Medicaid) and public education.

Third and finally, fiscal analysis of any kind of immigration should be placed within a consideration of the larger economic impact of immigrants. For example, the 2007 study undertaken by the comptroller of Texas that was just mentioned also estimated that the gross state product of Texas would drop by $17.7 billion if all 1.4 million Texan undocumented immigrants were deported.[80] This would result in a significant recession. A study in North Carolina on the impact of the Hispanic community, which was estimated to be half undocumented, found similar results.[81] In 2004, the Hispanic community was thought to be a $61,039,000 net cost to the state. However, the overall economic benefit of the community was noted to be substantial—a loss of the Hispanic community in construction alone would result in an estimated loss of $10 billion in value of construction, $2.7 billion in lost revenue for construction materials companies, and $149 million in revenue for companies renting buildings, machinery, and equipment.[82] The revenue from this construction generates substantial property taxes, corporate taxes, sales taxes, and income taxes for native-born employees in these industries that are virtually never factored into discussions of the fiscal impact of immigrants. In other words, while immigrants can be a tax burden on states, their larger economic benefits appear to more than offset this burden.

Where does this leave us? Unfortunately (as is now clear), indisputable answers and definitive dollar values for the fiscal effect of immigrants, undocumented immigrants, and refugees are difficult to attain. Some states like Texas clearly benefit

80 Strayhorn, *Undocumented Immigrants*, 20.
81 John D. Kasarda and James H. Johnson Jr., *The Economic Impact of the Hispanic Population on the State of North Carolina* (Chapel Hill, NC: Frank Hawkins Kenan Institute of Private Enterprise, 2006), ix.
82 Kasarda and Johnson, 28.

fiscally from those who illegally enter the state, while other states like California have a larger tax burden, though even this burden is offset within generations. Most of the fiscal burden appears to fall on states and local governments, while the federal government benefits according to many estimates, particularly in terms of social security and Medicare. When we factor in the economic growth produced by immigrants, and the tax revenue this growth produces, it seems that the direct fiscal loss of first-generation immigrants is considerably offset by the indirect fiscal benefits and by the direct benefits of their second- and third-generation descendants. While it is true that there are some additional costs associated with resettling refugees through UN resettlement programs, and that refugee participation in welfare programs may be high initially,[83] generally speaking, the cost to governmental budgets for welcoming refugees, asylum seekers, and nonconvention refugees is not large enough to justify the hostility that these migrants often face. As a whole, immigrants appear to benefit the federal government but are a fiscal burden on local governments.[84] Perhaps the main economic concern is not fiscal but related to wages, so I turn to consider that final economic factor.

Immigrants and Wages

A final major economic concern is that incoming refugees and asylum seekers will compete with citizens for jobs, resulting in lower wages. Here again, the results of studies depend partly on

---

83 Thomas Espenshade and Gregory Huber, "Fiscal Impacts of Immigrants and the Shrinking Welfare State," in Hirschman, Kasinitz, and Dewind, *Handbook of International Migration*, 361.
84 Espenshade and Huber, 361.

what is measured. Studies that focus on a smaller geographic location tend to find that immigrants have no impact on wages, but this may be because immigrants choose to move to cities that are already thriving economically or because natives move away upon their arrival.[85] George Borjas considered data nationwide and found that wages grew fastest in education and experience groups least affected by immigration.[86] Different studies, disagreeing on the extent to which slowing wage growth is due to immigration as opposed to other factors like capital growth, reach different estimates regarding the effect of immigration at a national level. One study suggests 3 percent wage growth lost for native workers; another suggests an initial loss of 0.4 percent wage growth but projects a 0.6 percent wage increase due to immigration in the long run.[87] Another study considered the effect of wages on excluding immigrants that had once been in the labor pool. Considering the elimination of the Bracero program, which had once brought seasonal agricultural laborers from Mexico, the study found that the termination of the program could not guarantee a rise in wages for citizen workers because bracero workers could simply be replaced with capital and technological changes.[88]

I turn now to consider the impact of refugees on labor markets in several European countries. A study of the Norwegian labor market from 1993 until 2006 estimated that immigration had a negative effect on wages and on days worked by day

85 George J. Borjas, *Immigration Economics* (Cambridge, MA: Harvard University Press, 2014), 90–91.
86 Borjas, 94.
87 For a brief survey of the literature, see Bernt Bratsberg et al., "Immigration Wage Effects by Origin," *Scandinavian Journal of Economics* 116, no. 2 (April 2014): 361.
88 Michael A. Clemens, Ethan G. Lewis, and Hannah M. Postel, "Immigration Restrictions as Active Labor Market Policy: Evidence from the Mexican Bracero Exclusion," *American Economic Review* 108, no. 6 (June 2018), 1468–87.

laborers, but most of this negative effect was due to migration from other Scandinavian countries and not from developing nations from which refugees would migrate.[89] Another study in Denmark considered workers from 1991 to 2008 as affected by a refugee dispersal policy from 1986 until 1998, as well as other migration flows. It found that refugees, who typically were not fluent in Danish and lacked more than a high school education, competed with less educated workers but that many of these workers were pushed into nonmanual occupations where they earned higher wages, estimating a 1–1.8 percent wage increase for each 1 percent growth in employment due to refugee arrivals.[90]

What about countries that may have a far more substantial refugee presence from a neighboring country? One recent study of Tanzania, a country that received numerous Rwandan and Burundian refugees in the 1990s, modeled the economic consequences of a new, average-size (i.e., 64,249 people) refugee camp being established in the country. Drawing on data obtained from fieldwork in Tanzania, the study estimated general economic growth due to increased consumption, resulting in higher wages, though both self-employed and agricultural sectors would benefit considerably less due to competition.[91] There are many more studies on this question, but these can serve as a representative selection.

89 Bratsberg et al., "Immigration Wage Effects," 382. Note that Norway already had the sixth highest ratio of refugees and asylees to the total population among European and North American countries from 1975 to 1992. See Gil Loescher and Ann Dull Loescher, *The Global Refugee Crisis: A Reference Handbook* (Santa Barbara, CA: ABC-CLIO, 1994), 83.

90 Mette Foged and Giovanni Peri, "Immigrants' Effect on Native Workers: New Analysis on Longitudinal Data," *American Economic Journal: Applied Economics* 8, no. 2 (2016): 3, 21.

91 Jean-François Maystadt and Philip Verwimp, "Winners and Losers among a Refugee-Hosting Population," *Economic Development and Cultural Change* 62, no. 4 (July 2014): 786–91.

When we consider the economic impact of refugees, we see that the picture is far murkier than when we considered the impact of refugees on crime and national security, though there is good reason to believe that the overall picture is still one of economic benefit. Wages may be suppressed by refugee and asylee arrivals but generally only in sectors where there is competition, typically in low-wage and often manual-labor fields. In some circumstances, this competition has resulted in natives shifting into more profitable work. Refugees are a tax burden on local governments and sometimes on states but generally help strengthen federal welfare programs like social security and Medicare. Their descendants typically earn more money and pay more taxes, often becoming a source of net revenue instead of a fiscal burden on the state. Once we factor in the economic growth that refugees and asylees help foster, it is not at all clear that the economic costs of welcoming asylees and refugees are substantial enough to justify the sorts of exclusion, deterrence, and abandonment that we see of refugees on a global scale.

Bearing False Testimony

While the data show that immigrants, including refugees and asylees, are not a security threat, media and politicians, among others, tend to depict them as dangerous forces. Otto Santa Ana studied how the *Los Angeles Times*, a progressive newspaper, covered immigration during debates surrounding the possible adoption of Proposition 187, a method of deterrence that would prohibit the provision of health care, education, and social services to undocumented immigrants. The dominant metaphors used for immigration in *Times* articles during this time were taken from war ("invasion," "siege," "takeover"—23.2 percent), disease (immigration causing "societal ills," Proposition 187 "curing" a "disease," etc.—8.8 percent), and especially, dangerous waters ("brown tide," "a sea of brown faces," "human surge," "inexorable flow," "flood"—58.2 percent).[92] Such negative imagery does not fit with the facts about immigration, crime, and the economy, especially since Proposition 187, debated in 1994, was responding to immigrants that had come to the United States in part due to US interventionist military policies in El Salvador and Guatemala or else from Mexico, as the recently signed North American Free Trade Agreement (NAFTA) was beginning to cause problems for Mexican employment levels. From the standpoint of many immigrants, the US government was no doubt the dangerous force that had helped empower a takeover of elected governments in their homelands.

The frequent misrepresentations of immigrants as criminals and a threat to the economy are exacerbated by persistent bigotry and racial discrimination from some Americans and Europeans, including politicians and other persons in authority. Such bigotry is found in the lowest levels of government, like Johnston County, North Carolina, where Sheriff Steve Bizzell condemned Mexicans as "trashy" and "breeding like rabbits."[93] It is found in state legislatures. Kristin Heyer notes an example from Kansas: "[In a] discussion about the problem of feral swine in Kansas, Rep. Virgil Peck (R-Tyro) suggested 'if shooting these immigrant feral hogs works, maybe we have found a (solution) to our illegal immigrant problem.'"[94] Such rhetoric is even found at the level of the US president, perhaps most notoriously

---

92 Otto Santa Ana, *Brown Tide Rising: Metaphors of Latinos in Contemporary American Public Discourse* (Austin: University of Texas Press, 2002), 69–74.

93 De La Torre, *Trails of Hope*, 116.

94 Kristin E. Heyer, *Kinship across Borders: A Christian Ethic of Immigration* (Washington, DC: Georgetown University Press, 2012), 140.

evident in Donald Trump's claims that "when Mexico sends its people, they're not sending their best. . . . They're sending people that have lots of problems, and they're bringing those problems with us. They're bringing drugs. They're bringing crime. They're rapists. And some, I assume, are good people."

The ancient Israelites were once scapegoated by the Egyptians as a national security threat (Exod 1:9–10), leading the Egyptians to fear and enslave the Israelites, even as they were dependent upon Israelite labor (e.g., Exod 5).[95] In a similar fashion, immigrants today are depicted as a threat, even as American agriculture, for example, needs foreign workers to ensure that all crops are harvested. As I read Matthew 2, I wonder whether Mary and Joseph feared similar scapegoating as they traveled toward Egypt. I wonder who assumed they might be criminals. I wonder where Joseph found work as a carpenter and whether he was paid fairly. I wonder if the Lord Jesus Christ was treated the way refugees are treated in the modern world.

---

95 This insightful point is made in Mark W. Hamilton, *Jesus, King of Strangers: What the Bible Really Says about Immigration* (Grand Rapids, MI: Eerdmans, 2019), 68.

6

Duty, Solidarity, and
Jesus the Refugee

I HAVE REACHED THE END of my exploration of what would happen to the holy family if they were seeking refuge under the current international refugee regime. As we have seen, the holy family would likely be denied refugee status because the best interpretation of their historical circumstances is that they are internally displaced migrants. If they sought to leave the borders of the Roman Empire to seek safety, they would likely face violent efforts to prevent their pursuit of asylum or else a denial of due process if they were able to cross a border in an effort to make an asylum claim. Even if they were able to make an asylum claim, there is a chance they would be unable to meet the burden of proof. Jesus, Mary, and Joseph may also have sought help in a refugee camp, where they would have likely remained without opportunities for employment, education, or resettlement. Alternately, the holy family could have chosen to settle in an urban setting as undocumented, which would have posed challenges in finding work and the perpetual risk of arrest and expulsion. Even supposing the holy family made it through all obstacles, they would still face potential prejudice and discrimination in their new country.

This thought experiment demands a Christian analysis of the international refugee regime. There is much to analyze, but a full corrective policy package would be too technical for a work of this nature.[1] For that reason, this chapter will instead focus on several more modest goals. First, I intend to demonstrate that Christians are called to solidarity with refugees in part because Jesus has identified himself with refugees. Second, recognizing that over eighty-two million displaced persons are currently in the world,[2] I will draw on the principles of restitution and relationship as a simple ethical framework to help identify which displaced persons have the clearest claims for aid from a given nation-state. Third, because solidarity, relationship, and restitution are not the only moral considerations relevant to the question of who ought to care for refugees and how, I will explore several objections and additional ethical principles that might seem to weigh against welcoming the refugee. Here, I will argue that the care of refugees, particularly ones to whom restitution is owed or relationship is present, bears greater moral weight than other moral considerations. Clearly, this chapter will be largely theoretical in nature, but chapter 7 will include a more practical analysis of solidarity for those seeking more concrete action steps.

---

1 Frankly, development of a full corrective policy package is also beyond the abilities of this author. I am an ethicist and theologian, not a political scientist or economist.
2 This UNHCR estimate includes IDPs, refugees, and asylees.

Solidarity with Refugees, Solidarity with Christ

A basic moral principle that serves as the bedrock of a Christian analysis of the refugee system is that of solidarity. In simple terms, solidarity is a coresponsibility between different groups of people based on their shared humanity, a "bearing with one another in love" (Eph 4:2).[3] Solidarity is rooted in the image of God, which all people bear (Gen 1:26–27). This concept lays important ethical foundations from the earliest chapters of Genesis.[4] Here, the democratized image of God that is extended to all humans stands in stark contrast with other ancient Near Eastern cultures, where the king alone might be God's image. It is because humans bear God's image that God can say creation is "very good" (Gen 1:31), and due to the image of God, murder is harshly condemned (Gen 9:6). The image of God demands at a basic level that we value the life of each human as good and treat the violent loss of human life as evil. For the Christian, solidarity is further amplified by ecclesiology. Because Christians proclaim the catholicity and universality of the church, we are required to stand in solidarity with all peoples, because each person is either actually or potentially a member of the body of Christ and so indispensable to us (1 Cor 12:21).[5] "If one part of the body suffers, all the parts suffer with it" (1 Cor 12:26). In its basic contours, then, solidarity calls us to use the gifts we have

---

3 I am influenced in this definition by Jon Sobrino, "Bearing with One Another in Faith," in *Theology of Christian Solidarity*, trans. Phillip Berryman (Maryknoll, NY: Orbis, 1985), 8, 10, 15, 16.

4 The outline of the image of God in ethics is helpfully presented in Patrick Nullens and Ronald T. Michener, *The Matrix of Christian Ethics: Integrating Philosophy and Moral Theology in a Postmodern Context* (Colorado Springs: Paternoster, 2010), 173–76.

5 Juan Hernández Pico, "Solidarity with the Poor and the Unity of the Church," in Berryman, *Theology of Christian Solidarity*, 80. Large numbers of refugees and asylees are actually Christian, not merely potential converts.

been given by God to preserve the life and prevent the suffering and death of all human beings while receiving from them their reciprocal care and the gifts that they have been given by God.

The general Christian call to solidarity with all people is made more pointed for certain categories of human beings, including migrants like refugees, asylees, and internally displaced persons. While some Mesopotamian codes of law speak of the need to care for the orphan and the widow, Deuteronomy speaks of care for the orphan, widow, *and migrant* (*gēr*; see Deut 14:29; 16:11, 14; 24:17–20; 26:12–13; 27:19).[6] In other ancient Near Eastern cultures, the immigrant is mentioned in law not as a special object of care but as a potentially puzzling challenge to property law and international affairs.[7] This biblical inclusion of migrants within vulnerable groups, which is unique to Israel, reveals the divine care given to migrants, challenging Christians to show solidarity to the same groups today.

The Old Testament emphasis on the migrant is also present in the New Testament, most notably in Jesus's parable of the sheep and the goats in Matthew 25:31–46. Jesus tells the parable as follows:

> But when the Son of Man comes in His glory, and all the angels with Him, then He will sit on His glorious throne. And all the nations will be gathered before Him; and He

---

6 Christiana Van Houten, *The Alien in Israelite Law*, Journal for the Study of the Old Testament Supplement Series 107 (Sheffield, UK: JSOT, 1991), 34–35.

7 M. Daniel Carroll R. explains that in other ancient Near Eastern law codes, "there are a few laws that deal with the marital and property rights of someone who leaves for a time and returns (Laws of Eshunna, §30; Laws of Hammurabi, §§30, 31, 136). Law 41 of the Laws of Eshunna refers to a foreigner who seems to be a merchant of some kind, but its interpretation is disputed. There were also stipulations in treaties and in correspondence between kingdoms regarding the possible obligations to return runaway slaves, free workers, or political refugees." M. Daniel Carroll R., *The Bible and Borders: Hearing God's Word on Immigration* (Grand Rapids, MI: Brazos, 2020), 65.

will separate them from one another, just as the shepherd separates the sheep from the goats; and He will put the sheep on His right, but the goats on the left.

Then the King will say to those on His right, "Come, you who are blessed of My Father, inherit the kingdom prepared for you from the foundation of the world. For I was hungry, and you gave Me something to eat; I was thirsty, and you gave Me something to drink; I was a stranger, and you invited Me in; naked, and you clothed Me; I was sick, and you visited Me; I was in prison, and you came to Me." Then the righteous will answer Him, "Lord, when did we see You hungry, and feed You, or thirsty, and give You something to drink? And when did we see You as a stranger, and invite You in, or naked, and clothe You? And when did we see You sick, or in prison, and come to You?" And the King will answer and say to them, "Truly I say to you, to the extent that you did it for one of the least of these brothers or sisters of Mine, you did it for Me."

Then He will also say to those on His left, "Depart from Me, you accursed people, into the eternal fire which has been prepared for the devil and his angels; for I was hungry, and you gave Me nothing to eat; I was thirsty, and you gave Me nothing to drink; I was a stranger, and you did not invite Me in; naked, and you did not clothe Me; sick, and in prison, and you did not visit Me." Then they themselves also will answer, "Lord, when did we see You hungry, or thirsty, or as a stranger, or naked, or sick, or in prison, and did not take care of You?" Then He will answer them, "Truly I say to you, to the extent that you did not do it for one of the least of these, you did not do it for Me, either." These will go away into eternal punishment, but the righteous into eternal life.

In this parable, Jesus identifies care for the "stranger" with care for himself. The Greek term used here is *Xenos*, which is typically translated as "stranger." When used in the Septuagint (the Greek translation of the Old Testament), it is occasionally used to translate *nokri* (foreigner) and, in one instance, to translate *gēr* (migrant).[8] This flexibility suggests that the term is *capacious*, and Jesus is indiscriminately calling for the care of immigrants, temporary migrants, and foreign visitors. There are commentators that interpret this passage differently, and I will treat their objections below, but I am convinced that the evidence requires that this passage be seen as a clear call to solidarity with strangers who need to be invited in, including refugees, asylees, and IDPs.

We in Europe and the United States have real reason to fear being the goats in this parable. Rather than welcoming Jesus through welcoming "strangers" or migrants, we are likely to sequester Jesus and the migrants in whom he is embodied in a refugee camp for years. Christ is daily turned back after being intercepted outside of our borders, sometimes violently. Many of those denied refugee status find themselves facing hunger, thirst, nakedness, sickness, and imprisonment, whether in private prisons in the United States where undocumented immigrants are processed or in the far more gruesome prisons of Libya, which enslave would-be asylees before they reach Europe. For many in the West, our general failure of solidarity is not malicious; often, we

---

8 *Xenos* translates *nokri* five times (2 Sam 15:19; Ps 69:8; Ruth 2:10; Lam 5:2; Eccl 6:2) and *gēr* once (Job 31:32).

are simply unaware of the situation facing such refugees.[9] We do not visit, clothe, and care for such migrants because we do not know that they exist. For those who do know about the refugee crisis, it is important to consider where to begin showing solidarity to refugees and, through the fulfillment of such moral responsibilities, solidarity with Christ.

Clarifying Solidarity

While the Bible is clear that we ought to show solidarity to migrants, were the argument to stop here, it would be inadequate. As Tisha Rajendra explains, "Without assigning who has the duty to [care] for which groups of impoverished and vulnerable people," arguments that appeal to universal duties fail "to account for why a particular group of people should take responsibility for a particular group of needy and vulnerable poor."[10] In other words, without further argument, a general appeal to solidarity may still leave refugees without recognition and/or protection because it is possible for numerous countries to recognize a general responsibility to show solidarity to refugees while each country assumes another country has the particular responsibility to care for a given group. In this case, that given group may be entirely without care, despite the general consensus that they are owed care and protection.

---

9 Even as I began researching a book on the subject of refugees, after having taught on the subject for several years and having served and worked with refugees and asylees in several different cities, much of the information that I discovered was surprising to me. I do not exempt myself from the common lack of information among many Americans.

10 Rajendra, *Migrants and Citizens*, 26. In her argument, Rajendra specifically addressed arguments from the universal nature of human rights and from the preferential option for the poor, but my appeal to solidarity faces similar objections.

At this point in the argument, a threefold distinction provided by David Owen helps clarify our duties to refugees. Owen distinguishes between "general responsibility," which all participants in the international order have toward refugees; "particular responsibility," which arises from a specific relationship with a given refugee; and "special responsibility," which follows from actions that a given state may take that contribute to the causes of the refugee's flight.[11] The call to solidarity with refugees that is rooted in our common humanity and amplified by the parable of the sheep and the goats is one way of specifying our general responsibility to refugees. However, many countries have particular and/or special responsibilities to refugees that extend beyond these general responsibilities. In this section, I will explore the particular responsibility arising from a preestablished relationship and the special responsibility due to the obligation to provide restitution. Taken together, these responsibilities help clarify which refugee groups should receive care from which countries.

Relationships and Particular Responsibility to Refugees

In the words of Tisha Rajendra, justice requires "responsibility to relationships."[12] As Rajendra notes, one of the shortcomings of many ethical analyses of immigration is that immigrant rights are clearly explained, but the question of who has the duty to secure these rights is typically neglected.[13] Without assigning particular responsibility, refugees are often left unprotected. David Owen clarifies the situation, noting that care for refugees

---

11 David Owen, *What Do We Owe to Refugees?* (Medford, MA: Polity, 2020), 86–88.
12 Rajendra, *Migrants and Citizens*, 7.
13 Rajendra, 12, 76.

is often rooted in an "ideology of humanitarianism," viewing care as a generous gift rather than a duty of justice.[14] As long as we interpret solidarity with refugees as an act of charity, a humanitarian act, then our solidarity will seem like something that is done above the requirements of justice, an optional and gracious gift to those in need. A closer examination of justice reveals that the paradigm of humanitarianism is insufficient.

The relational nature of justice can be established in various ways, but I will begin with a biblical emphasis. The Hebrew *ṣedeq*, meaning "justice," is a relational term, often set in the context of a covenant relationship. As Christopher Wright explains, "For Israel the whole idea of justice was wrapped up with the qualities and characteristics of the Lord, their God, and especially connected to the covenant relationship between Israel and the Lord. Justice is essentially relational and covenantal."[15] The Old Testament sought to explain the relationship between the *gēr* (which can be translated as "sojourner," "stranger," or "migrant") and the Israelite in terms suggesting a duty of care for family, such that establishing a relationship with a migrant resulted in all the duties one might have toward family. For example, Deuteronomy 24:14–15 puts "your brothers-sisters" parallel to "your stranger," which Mark and Luke Glanville suggest is intended "to enfold the stranger within Deuteronomy's brother-sister ethic." The stranger is on equal footing with the Israelite in terms of the claims of justice.[16] More surprisingly, Israel's treatment of migrants is sometimes used as a benchmark

---

14 David Owen, "Refugees and the Politics of Indignity," in Oliver, *Refugees Now*, 18–19.

15 Christopher J. H. Wright, *Old Testament Ethics for the People of God* (Downers Grove, IL: InterVarsity Academic, 2004), 258–59.

16 Glanville and Glanville, *Refuge Reimagined*, 30. The Glanvilles go further: "Deuteronomy's vision for the stranger is that she or he is to be grafted into the household, the clan, and the nation" (39).

for how one ought to treat family. Leviticus 25:35–36 teaches that if kin fall on hard times, the Israelites should treat them as if they are strangers and let them be supported. Again, Mark and Luke Glanville explain, "The words 'as though they were strangers' display a cultural norm: Israelite households were used to enfolding and caring for impoverished strangers. . . . Foreigners were so protected that the way Israel treats strangers is the benchmark for how they are to treat the poor!"[17] Scripture clearly conceives of justice in relational terms and prioritizes relationships established with migrants.

Here is where Rajendra's insights into the relational nature of justice are particularly helpful: when—through colonialism, international financial investment, or intentional guest worker programs—a nation establishes a relation manifest in transnational migratory routes in the manner explained by migration-systems theory, that nation has a corresponding duty to immigrants and refugees who might follow this migratory route. This principle makes sense for several reasons. First, existing migration routes, which are one form of relation between cultures, provide a framework within which a refugee can reasonably and more safely travel to a new home. Second, the existence of such migratory routes means that many refugees will have family, friends, or coworkers in the recipient country. If we must make decisions about whom to help with limited time and resources, it is prudent that decisions will prioritize those who are already known at a personal level. The duty to care for family is especially pertinent here. Third, because an existing migratory route means that transnational connections already exist, refugees will more quickly be able to acclimate to the recipient country because translation services, community

---

17 Glanville and Glanville, 54.

support, and personal connections to help navigate new legal structures may all be present.[18]

Speaking from personal experience, I can say that progress in developing the basic language skills necessary to pursue a job is very slow when there is no one present who knows one's native language. I once volunteered as an English-as-a-second-language tutor for a Burmese refugee family, but I did not know their native language. I would visit the family's home and point to objects, repeating the relevant English words. Otherwise, members of the family would repeat actions I performed while saying the English word for these actions. Their progress was incredibly slow because I was never able to answer questions or even confirm that they rightly understood how the words they were repeating correlated with the objects I pointed to or actions I demonstrated. For example, once the father in the family, who was always incredibly generous, offered me a plate of mango, bananas, and oranges, saying the Burmese word for the items so that I could tell him the English equivalent. But was he sharing the Burmese word for snack, fruit, gift, or one of the specific fruits? How could I be certain my translation was accurate? Much more effective integration would have been possible if I had even basic language proficiency in Burmese, which shows how it can be easier for refugees who follow existing migration patterns toward communities where some individuals already speak their language. It is clear to me that existing relationships are a clear basis for identifying which community ought to prioritize solidarity with which group of refugees.

---

18 On the role that available translation resources play in nonprofit efficacy in resettlement, see Bauman, Soerens, and Smeir, *Seeking Refuge*, 92–93.

Restitution and Special Responsibility to Refugees

In the words of Serena Parekh, "Western states are too often seen only as *rescuers* and not as in part responsible for the inability of refugees to find refuge."[19] While we often think of our support of refugees as a positive duty (e.g., a duty to do good), in fact, much support of refugees could also be characterized as part of our negative duties (e.g., a duty to avoid doing harm).[20] While hospitality is certainly an important virtue, as Miguel De La Torre reminds us, "The virtue of hospitality masks the complexity caused by the consequences of empire building."[21] Perhaps we see ourselves as those who can welcome strangers and who will be identified as sheep in the final judgment, when in some instances, we might be better characterized as partly responsible for their plight, identified as goats in the judgment, or worse. This possibility necessitates a discussion of special responsibilities.

Special responsibilities to refugees are not considered frequently enough in much public discourse about immigration. In such discourse, refugees can often accrue a sort of "invisible debt," meaning that refugees who owe their security, safety, and very presence to the host country may feel a power imbalance and a dependency in terms of social indebtedness.[22] However, it is sometimes the host nation that has a debt to the refugee. This is evident in what Serena Parekh helpfully calls the "you -break-it-you-bought-it principle"—if you cause the damage to

---

19 Parekh, *No Refuge*, 17.

20 As Parekh notes, a negative duty is "generally considered stronger and more demanding—the rescuers cannot be asked to sacrifice too much" (18).

21 De La Torre, *Immigration Crisis*, 159.

22 On the concept of invisible debt, see Ilsup Ahn, *Religious Ethics and Migration: Doing Justice to Undocumented Workers* (New York: Routledge, 2014), 21–25.

a country leading to flight, you have a special responsibility to the refugees who flee as a result of your actions.[23] Restitution has been a principle of Christian ethics for centuries. For example, Thomas Aquinas writes that commutative justice "is impossible, unless he that has less than his due receive what is lacking to him; and for this to be done, restitution must be made to the person from whom a thing has been taken."[24] In the case of refugees, if a nation is responsible even in part for their loss of safety, property, political rights, or health, then that nation has a duty of restitution to the refugees in question. Aquinas even argued, partly on the basis of Romans 1:32, that those complicit in destructive acts by consent, by participation in the rewards of the destructive act, or by neglect to prevent the act are obligated to provide restitution.[25] In other words, even if most Americans had no direct role in American interventionism that contributed to the production of Haitian or Salvadoran refugees, if they supported politicians who pursued interventionism, if they benefited economically or in terms of national security from such intervention, or if they failed to object to such intervention, then restitution is owed.

Long before the Middle Ages, the Biblical vision of justice included a requirement for restitution to those you have harmed. The Hebrew ṣᵉdāqâ, the standard term for justice in the Old Testament, is multifaceted in meaning. The term is not restricted to punitive measures. It often includes a notion of the need to correct oppression.[26] In itself, this facet of the

---

23 Parekh, *No Refuge*, 80.
24 Thomas Aquinas, *Summa Theologica*, trans. Fathers of the Dominican Province (Allen, TX: Christian Classics, 1948), II-II Q. 62 a. 5.
25 Aquinas, II-II Q. 62 a. 7.
26 Stephen Charles Mott, *Biblical Ethics and Social Change* (Oxford: Oxford University Press, 1982), 63, 71.

term's meaning orients biblical justice toward care for the poor and oppressed, which would include a concern for refugees. When justice is explored in the context of a violent or nonviolent offense against a person, penal provisions might include both retribution (e.g., the provision of a fitting punishment) and restitution (e.g., compensation for loss), where both restitution and retribution ought to be proportional to the offense (see Deut 19:18–20 and 25:1–3).[27] The famous lex talionis—"eye for eye, tooth for tooth, hand for hand, and foot for foot" (Deut 19:20)—is actually a means of ensuring proportionate retribution and restitution.[28] At times, victims' relatives might be able to seek restitution in the form of compensation for damages rather than simply seeking retributive punishment (Exod 21:30; Lev 24:18; Num 35:31–32).[29] In other instances, only restitution is named (Exod 21:33–36; 22:5–14; Num 5:5–10). Though less central, restitution continues as a theme in the New Testament, perhaps most notably in the story of the conversion of Zacchaeus (Luke 19:1–10), who not only manifested justice by giving half of his possessions to the poor, showing favor to the oppressed, but also promised a fourfold restitution to anyone he had extorted (Luke 19:8). While Christians may be challenged to embody mercy by forgoing the pursuit of retribution through the lex talionis (Matt 5:38–40), they are still encouraged to make things right with a

---

27 Wright, *Old Testament Ethics*, 310; Cyril S. Rodd, *Glimpses of a Strange Land: Studies in Old Testament Ethics* (Edinburgh: T&T Clark, 2001), 129–30.

28 Wright, *Old Testament Ethics*, 310; Richard H. Hiers, *Justice and Compassion in Biblical Law* (New York: Continuum, 2009), 152.

29 Hiers, *Justice and Compassion*, 151. Hiers notes that the Numbers text's prohibition on compensation instead of retribution for a murderer suggests that such a substitution might be acceptable in other criminal categories.

sister or brother they have wronged (Matt 5:23–26), which presumably could include restitution.[30]

There are many possible examples of foreign intervention that might require restitution. For example, the United States is in the peculiar position of being one of the world's leaders in refugee resettlement while also being one of a handful of countries whose military actions have contributed to large portions of displaced migrants. Ethicists and policy analysts point to US support of the Mujahideen in Afghanistan or its training of the elite Salvadoran Atlacatl Battalion, which killed 936 villagers in the Morazán province, mostly at the village of El Mozote, as examples of situations where the United States bears some responsibility of restitution for the harms that refugees, asylees, and IDPs have faced.[31] For present purposes, I will return to an example mentioned in chapter 1. We see a clear example of Parekh's principle in the example of Nicaraguan refugees in La Carpio, Costa Rica. Since 1934, the Somoza family had controlled Nicaragua, and the United States had viewed them as allies against the expansion of communism in Central America during the Cold War. Part of this American support involved the United States training the Nicaraguan National Guard, the same national guard that was responsible for assassinating thirty thousand political opponents prior to 1972. Such assassinations were partly aimed at preserving extreme wealth inequalities—the Somoza family alone owned one-third of the nation's land, while US corporations owned thousands more acres and controlled

---

30 The fact that the passage encourages settling on the way to court suggests that the offense is somehow subject to retribution or restitution. If they do not settle, they will be thrown into prison and "will not be released until [they] have paid the last penny" (Matt 5:26), clarifying that restitution is at least partly in mind.

31 Consider the perspectives of the following historians, ethicists, and policy analysts: García, *Seeking Refuge*, 24; Ishay, *History of Human Rights*, 290; Dakin-Grimm, *Dignity and Justice*, 17–26; and De La Torre, *Immigration Crisis*, 20–33.

the mining, lumber, banking, and railroad industries. In the face of such inequality, the Sandinista National Liberation Front (FSLN) began a war against the government. The government responded by increasing surveillance and torture of its citizens and by denying the right to free press and speech. Eventually, US support ended during the Jimmy Carter administration, and the Somoza administration soon fell. When it did, the Ronald Reagan administration backed the contras (*contra-revolucionarios*) in attempts to overthrow the Sandinistas. A CIA training manual released in the press showed that contras were being trained in sabotage, kidnapping, and murder.[32] In this situation, the you-break-it-you-bought-it principle would require the United States to offer some form of restitution to those harmed or at risk of harm.

Of course, not all refugees will want to accept aid from those countries that have a special responsibility to provide it. Consider the example of an unnamed Salvadoran refugee. She explains that the civil wars in Nicaragua and Guatemala in the 1980s were inspired by Marxism, leading the United States to characterize the concurrent war in El Salvador as "part of a big political domino—part of the Cold War game between the United States and communist Russia."[33] While President Jimmy Carter was supplying guns, helicopters, and intelligence to the Salvadoran government, soldiers from the same government raided her community, performing mass rapes and executions, even throwing babies into the air and using them for target practice.[34] Eventually, her father, a politician sympathetic to land reform, was murdered. "Knowing what the United States had done to

---

32 García, *Seeking Refuge*, 14–19.
33 Ivaylo Grouev, ed., *Bullets on the Water: Refugee Stories* (London: McGill-Queen's University Press, 2000), 69–70.
34 Grouev, 71.

[her] country," she did not want to seek asylum there, even though several family members became undocumented workers there. In her words, "I don't have anything against the Americans, but I cannot stand their politics of backing obedient dictators from Central America. They do not care about democracy and human rights."[35] She pursued asylum in Canada, receiving it and being resettled there. Such stories show the clear special responsibility the United States had to noncombatant victims of the government it was arming while also revealing the personal decisions that complexify these responsibilities. Some will want nothing to do with a country that owes them restitution; others will seek aid from such a country, even when that country has no intention of providing restitution, forcing those owed such restitution to become undocumented. Fulfillment of special responsibilities will therefore take various forms, from direct acceptance of resettlement to subsidizing the resettlement efforts of neutral third parties like Canada. However the specifics are resolved, it is clearly the case that special responsibilities exist and clarify the priorities of nation-states seeking to identify which refugees should receive their focused care.

Considering the Counterpoints

Having made a brief case for our responsibility to refugees, I turn now to consider reasons why some may find my argument unconvincing. This survey is not exhaustive, but I hope it will cover most major objections and alternative interpretations of the Christian response to the international refugee regime and the hypothetical plight of Jesus the refugee. I begin with direct objections to the argument I have made before moving to

---

35 Grouev, 73.

consider alternative ethical principles that might be thought to resist any call for increased acceptance of refugees and/or asylees.

Objection to My Reading of Matthew 25:31–46

One objection to my argument so far is that my appeal to the parable of the sheep and the goats is not convincing because it does not refer to migrants. Some interpreters deny that Matthew 25:31–46 speaks of Jesus's solidarity with all those who need provision and welcome. This objection tends to focus on the specific terminology used to speak of those in need. Thus, James Hoffmeier argues, "The New Testament nowhere refers to all humanity as 'brothers of Jesus,'" the term used of the needy in Matthew 25:40.[36] Rather, this term tends to be used to speak of Jesus's disciples, as it typically is in Matthew (see 12:48–49; 28:10). Similarly, R. T. France notes that the phrase "these least ones" (Matt 25:41), which describes the needy in the parable of the sheep and the goats, is also used to refer to Jesus's disciples in Matthew (see 10:42; 18:6, 10, 14).[37] On this basis, and given the fact that many of the early disciples were destitute (1 Cor 1:26–29) and were sent without provisions and instructed to seek care from others (Matt 10:9–15), some conclude that in the parable of the sheep and the goats, Jesus is teaching that one treats Jesus as they treat his representatives, who happen to be poor.[38]

---

36 Hoffmeier, *Immigration Crisis*, 149.

37 R. T. France, *The Gospel of Matthew* (Grand Rapids, MI: Eerdmans, 2007), 958.

38 Craig Keener situates this within the context of Matt 10:40–42, where the one who gives water to "one of these little ones to drink because he is a disciple" is rewarded, and whoever receives the disciples receives Christ. Craig S. Keener, *A Commentary on the Gospel of Matthew* (Grand Rapids, MI: Eerdmans, 1999), 605. Even if this interpretation is valid, Bauman, Soerens, and Smeir note that many refugees, asylum seekers, and nonconvention refugees are Christian and thus would fall under this parable's ethical mandate. Bauman, Soerens, and Smeir, *Seeking Refuge*, 37–42. See also Zehnder, *Bible and Immigration*, 84.

While I can understand why some scholars adopt this interpretation, I do not find it convincing for several reasons. First, the sheep and the goats are both surprised: "When did we see you a stranger and welcome you, or naked and clothe you?" (Matt 25:38).[39] It was commonly understood that a commissioned representative of an agent bore that individual's authority (Matt 10:40–42; John 13:20), so the surprise of the sheep and the goats suggests that the needy in the passage were not known as disciples.[40] Second, it may not be true that the New Testament never uses "brothers" (*adelphoi*) for those who are not disciples. Consider Matthew 5:22: "Whoever is angry with his brother shall be liable to judgment, and whoever says to his brother 'Raqa' will be answerable to the Sanhedrin." Arguably, this passage is using the term *brother* as synonymous with *neighbor*, showing that Matthew 25 might have a more general meaning of the word *brothers* rather than limiting the word to the disciples.[41] Besides, as I have noted earlier, Deuteronomy 24:14–15 does seem to fold the migrant into the family ethic of the Old Testament nation of Israel, suggesting that the new covenant family might adopt a similar approach. Third, the parable of the sheep and the goats discusses a wide range of situations of need. Some of these

---

39 See France, *Gospel of Matthew*, 959, 964. Note, however, that this argument does not persuade France that Jesus is speaking of all the needy rather than merely of disciples (959).

40 Here I interpret the principle of the agent (*shaliach*) as bearing the authority of the sender in the opposite manner of Lamar Cope, who sees this principle as evidence for interpreting "the least of these" as disciples. If the principle was culturally pervasive, Jesus's judgment of those who did not show care to his disciples would be expected, not a surprise. Cf. Lamar Cope, "Matthew XXV:31–46: 'The Sheep and the Goats' Reinterpreted," *Novum Testamentum* 11, nos. 1/2 (January–April 1969): 40.

41 Glanville and Glanville, *Refuge Reimagined*, 90. The significance of the language of "brothers and sisters" might be mitigated within the pericope as well. Nolland offers the unusual hypothesis that the absence of *tōn adelphōn* ("brothers and sisters") in Matt 25:45 suggests that disciples are only in view in v. 40, while v. 45 shows a wider solidarity with the poor. John Nolland, *The Gospel of Matthew* (Grand Rapids, MI: Eerdmans, 2005), 1033–34.

situations, such as travelers needing welcome and prisoners needing a visit, fit the context of itinerant Christian missionaries facing persecution and arrest. However, the situation of being sick or naked does not correlate specifically with what would be the expected circumstances of Jesus's disciples. Fourth, Jesus makes a similar statement in Mark 9:27, saying, "Whoever welcomes one such child in my name welcomes me." In this case, it is clear that Jesus is literally speaking about a child, whom he has just called over (Mark 9:26), identifying himself with another vulnerable category from Scripture. This similar story raises the likelihood that Jesus is speaking of literal strangers in the parable of the sheep and the goats. Such New Testament evidence weakens the case of Hoffmeier, France, and others, making it unclear whether Jesus is speaking about his disciples or about broader categories of people in need.

Even if the disciple Matthew does not intend to speak of Jesus's solidarity with all those in need, including all strangers who need welcome, when he records this parable, the basic features of such an interpretation can be proven entirely from the Old Testament. The Old Testament is unique in its mandate to care for the migrant. As discussed previously, Deuteronomy speaks of care for the migrant (*gēr*; see Deut 14:29; 16:11, 14; 24:17–20; 26:12–13; 27:19) in a manner atypical for its historical and cultural context.[42] As is typical of many laws in the Torah, laws about strangers in the land often have a "motivation clause" that explains why the people of Israel should obey the law. On several occasions, Deuteronomy includes what Christiana Van Houten calls a "promise of divine blessing," by which those who care for strangers will be blessed by God (see Deut 14:29;

---

42 Van Houten, *Alien in Israelite Law*, 34–35.

24:19, 21; cf. Jer 7:5–7).[43] Conversely, on several occasions, the prophets promise divine judgment for those who do not care for strangers in the land (see Ezek 16:49; 22:28–31; Mal 3:5). More than that, Old Testament wisdom literature has precedent for the idea that God is in solidarity with the poor: the one who cares for the poor "honors" and "lends to the Lord," while those who "oppress the poor revile their maker" (Prov 14:31; 19:17). Given that the poor are often especially represented by the trio of orphan, widow, and migrant (*gēr*),[44] it is not too far of a development to imagine God in solidarity with the migrant. Clearly, it is biblical to think that we will be judged or rewarded on the basis of our treatment of the poor and the stranger as if we had done such to God, even if it is somewhat unclear how such judgment fits with our concepts of justification by faith.[45] In light of Matthew 2:13–15, it is reasonable to add that these ideas fit Matthew's text given that Christ and his family once sought refuge and needed welcome too. Therefore, even if the human author of the Gospel of Matthew only intended to urge care for Christ's disciples as they migrated on evangelistic journeys (a contestable interpretation), according to what was traditionally named the *moral* or *tropological* sense of Scripture, it is valid to infer from the text a duty to stand in solidarity with immigrants, including

---

43 Van Houten, 168.

44 Besides the numerous examples in Deuteronomy cited earlier, see also Pss 94:6; 146:9; Jer 22:3; Ezek 22:7; Zech 7:10; and Mal 3:5.

45 This is a point of discussion and sometimes contention between Protestant and Catholic theologians. Indeed, in modern ecumenical debate, it is commonly noted that Catholic theology speaks of human merit precisely because of such language of reward and punishment in the final judgment. For more on this, see Susan K. Wood, "Catholic Reception of the Joint Declaration on the Doctrine of Justification," in *Rereading Paul Together: Protestant and Catholic Perspectives on Justification*, ed. David E. Aune (Grand Rapids, MI: Baker Academic, 2006), 48–49.

refugees and asylees.[46] At the level of Scripture's inspiration by the Holy Spirit, its divine authorship, a necessary moral implication of Matthew 25 in canonical context is the need to care for those in need, including refugees.[47]

Objections to Restitution

Given the fact that the special responsibility of restitution is a central facet of my understanding of our responsibilities to refugees, it is important to consider several possible objections to this principle. As David Miller argues, reparations often take the form of replacing what is damaged, so the right to immigrate may not be demanded by the principle of restitution in an immediate,

---

46 The medieval Latin Church was especially prone to seek a spiritual sense that went beyond the historico-grammatical meaning of the text based on their recognition that the Bible was inspired by God and therefore capable of containing meanings that went beyond what a historical author might consciously know. The best examples of medieval use of the spiritual senses of Scripture—which included the moral, allegorical, and anagogical senses—required that the spiritual meaning also be taught explicitly as a literal level elsewhere in the canon, as is the case here. No valid moral sense can contradict the literal. For more on the fourfold sense, see Ian Christopher Levy, *Introducing Medieval Biblical Interpretation: The Senses of Scripture in Premodern Exegesis* (Grand Rapids, MI: Baker, 2018), 33–34, 46, 190–94.

47 Here, Markus Zehnder offers an additional peculiar interpretation that serves as an objection. If "my brothers" is universal and not just restricted to Christians, Zehnder argues that "the text cannot be used to argue for any kind of one-sided agenda. In the present context, this also applies for a one-sided focus on support for (im)migrants . . . rather, the passage would suggest that help is extended evenly and not to one group at the expense of others" (86). This convoluted reasoning ignores that the judgment is based on who cares for the hungry, thirsty, naked, stranger, sick, and imprisoned, not based on how one treats the full, satisfied, clothed, family member of good health who serves as prison warden. Certainly, ideas like the image of God demand high levels of ethical treatment of all individuals, but to read the parable of the sheep and the goats in this way while ignoring the specifics leading to judgment in the text is unwarranted. The most charitable reading of Zehnder I can offer is that he is gesturing toward the alleged harm done to poor citizens by the arrival of immigrants, a harm that I have extensively challenged in chapter 5. A less charitable reading is that this is pure eisegesis. See Zehnder, *Bible and Immigration*, 86.

obvious way.[48] Perhaps in such circumstances, the interventionist nation could provide economic relief to those harmed by foreign involvement, for example. This sense of proportionality has a biblical sensibility to it, though this is not something Miller himself explores. As we have seen, the Old Testament lex talionis and other Deuteronomic laws (e.g., Deut 25:1–2) certainly are meant to ensure proportionality where the restitution or, in some cases, punishment fits the loss.[49] In many instances, what is lost is the safety associated with a homeland where basic rights to life, property, and freedoms of religion, speech, and assembly are protected. In the case of persecution by one's homeland, clearly, the loss is total, and the only possible resolution for a convention refugee is to escape to a new place of residence. However, even many IDPs and nonconvention refugees—such as Iraqis or Afghans who worked with the United States and who face a threat to their lives, liberties, or livelihoods as a result—would merit restitution that provides such safety in another context. It seems nearly impossible to guarantee the security of an individual who is a US ally in many postoccupation nations. Despite this, public opinion polls from the 1940s until the 1970s reveal consistent opposition to increasing refugee admissions among North American and European countries, even where there might be a direct moral duty of reparation, as is the case with the United States toward Vietnamese refugees. Despite this duty, polls found that a majority of Americans were opposed to increasing refugee

---

48 David Miller, *Strangers in Our Midst: The Political Philosophy of Immigration* (Cambridge, MA: Harvard University Press, 2016), 114. Miller admits that where persecution is present, resettling refugees may be the only means of amelioration, but this is not obviously the case in other categories considered, such as among nonconvention refugees, IDPs, or economic migrants.
49 See Hiers, *Justice and Compassion*, 152.

resettlement from Vietnam.[50] Even where public opinion seems more favorable, as with support for Afghan special immigrant visa holders, who had largely helped US forces in Afghanistan, the Biden administration's accelerated withdrawal of US forces from Afghanistan left many behind and failed to fulfill the duty of restitution.[51] Since refugees have largely lost a safe living environment where their rights are secured, restitution of such an environment by foreign nations whose interventionist policies disabled a refugee's homeland seems a proportionate restoration.

Other objections can be dealt with in a more rapid manner. Serena Parekh notes herself that if a country causes damage to another country for a good cause such that the creation of refugees is unintended, there may seem to be less obligation for restitution.[52] At first glance, this seems reasonable, but clarification is necessary. Intent is certainly relevant to considerations of criminality and hence of determining whether punishment is necessary for those who might damage the economy, political stability, or health and life of another country and its citizens, but damages for restitution can be owed even under accidental circumstances or due to negligence (Exod 22:5, 14). Consider another objection: some might argue that it is difficult to establish the proportionate responsibility of various nations in complex international affairs. For example, political instability in Afghanistan is a by-product of Afghani and transnational groups like the Taliban, Al Qaida, and the Islamic State, as well as of the coalition

---

50 Lewis M. Stern, "Response to Vietnamese Refugees: Surveys of Public Opinion," *Social Work* 26, no. 4 (July 1981): 306–11.

51 According to one Pew Research Poll, 56 percent of Americans support welcoming Afghan refugees. Pew Research, "Liberal Democrats Most Likely to Favor Admitting Refugees from Afghanistan," September 23, 2021, https://www.pewresearch.org/politics/2021/09/23/biden-administrations-handling-of-afghanistan-and-views-of-accepting-afghan-refugees-in-the-u-s/pp_2021-09-23_biden-approval_03-02/.

52 Parekh, *No Refuge*, 81.

of nations invading after 9/11 and of older warfare, such as that between the USSR and Afghanistan. Under such circumstances, how would we ascertain which group had the largest responsibility for restitution? In response, I must clarify that I am using the principle of restitution, or the you-break-it-you-bought-it principle, as a means of clarifying the general call to solidarity that Christians have toward all refugees in all contexts. As such, the principle of restitution is meant to identify those persons and groups of persons to whom there is a priority to show solidarity. I intend this as an initial call to action rather than as a means by which we can shirk our larger moral duty of welcoming the refugee as if she were Christ. Many refugees wait in refugee camps for a decade or more or else are repulsed at securitized borders. Any of the many nations with a duty to restitution for Afghanis could and should act to rectify this situation. Finally, some might object that welcoming refugees from war-torn areas, particularly those in which a nation has been involved militarily, is a recipe risking terrorism. As argued in chapter 5, however, I consider this risk inflated when proper security screening protocols are in place.

I have argued that there is a clear duty of restitution for harms done by potential receiving nations to refugee-producing nations and that this duty should lead to increased reception of refugees (both convention and nonconvention) and asylees. This does not abrogate the duty of reparations that a refugee-producing state may owe to its own citizens when the time may come for repatriation,[53] but it does help us identify areas where the European Union and United States can improve in their care

---

[53] For more on this, see Owen, *What Do We Owe*, 74–76, 83.

of refugees as a first step toward reforming the international refugee regime.

Appeal to the Right to Self-Determination

Sometimes a nation's particular responsibilities to refugees are weighed against a nation's right to self-determination, with the greater weight given to self-determination. For example, Michael Walzer points to the need to consider "ideological as well as ethnic affinity" when evaluating particular responsibility toward refugees. He gives the example of the 1956 anticommunist revolution in Hungary, a failed effort to overturn the communist government. Suppose that the effort had won, Walzer proposes. Would the United States have then had a duty to welcome communist refugees from Hungary?[54] This example suggests that a country may have good reasons for denying entry to asylees or refugees on the basis of the right to self-determination and a desire to preserve the national culture and ideology.

If we turn away from counterfactuals, like the hypothetical United States' need to welcome Hungarian communists, and consider the refugees who actually have been and are being turned away by the European Union and United States, the objection on the basis of self-determination is not as clearly applicable. In chapter 4, for example, I explored the case of extraterritorial interception of Haitian refugees by the United States and the resulting denial of due process by preventing full asylum hearings. According to census data, by the year 2000, there were over six hundred thousand Americans who identified

---

54 Michael Walzer, *Spheres of Justice: A Defense of Pluralism and Equality* (New York: Basic Books, 1983), 49.

as Haitian, and there is reason to believe that this estimate may be low.[55] Any attempt to deter Haitian immigrants in the name of self-determination assumes that the "self" doing the determining is not already constituted in part by Haitians. In other words, we must imagine that the American body politic is relatively homogenous racially, culturally, and socially to argue that the admission of further Haitians would somehow undermine American culture and values. In truth, Haitians already shape American culture in various ways, and they do so in large part because Americans have established a relationship with Haiti first through colonial conquest and later through international economic ties, ranging from development and aid to the presence of American business interests. It is on the basis of such ties that the United States has a particular responsibility to Haitian asylees and refugees. Where a nation has established an existing relationship with another country or people group, that relationship adds a layer of responsibility toward refugees and asylees that may leave that nation.

Some readers may not be convinced. Even granting that a people group is already present in the United States, might it be the case that something about a given group's culture could be damaging to a recipient culture, warranting efforts to prevent further immigration from members of that group? Here, two arguments provide additional warrant. The first is an appeal to common grace, the idea that God is graciously restraining sin in all cultures while enabling each culture to manifest goodness, beauty, and truth in different ways.[56] In the context of immigration, the doctrine of common grace means that all peoples and

---

55 Konczal and Stepik, "Haiti," 446–47.
56 For a short analysis of common grace, see Herman Bavinck, "Common Grace," trans. Raymond C. Van Leeuwen, *Calvin Theological Journal* 24, no. 1 (April 1989): 35–65.

cultures will have something to contribute to the common good. Matthew Kaemingk's work in the ethics of immigration shows that this principle can be used to defend a pluralistic vision of society that welcomes immigrants from different cultures without requiring full cultural homogeneity.[57] Because of common grace, there can never be certainty about where points of conflict or points of consensus may be found between a given migrant group and a recipient culture.[58] The mere existence of common grace prohibits our viewing of any culture or people as only a threat.

Recognizing that many refugee groups share a culture that is already contributing to American and European cultures and recognizing that common grace means that any culture or people can make positive contributions to any society, there is admittedly still a degree of risk. Some refugee groups might have political values, expected family roles, or religious beliefs that are contrary to those that I prefer as a Christian. No doubt refugee groups view aspects of my faith and culture as a risk as well. Nevertheless, as Christians committed to the Bible, we have good biblical reason to accept risk. Recognizing that individual verses taken out of canonical context can lead to a skewed ethic, Richard Hays has sought to develop "focal images" that summarize central themes of New Testament ethics. To count as a focal image, several criteria must be met. A focal image must be significant in the full range of New Testament texts, and it must not imbalance New Testament teaching by ignoring or decentering alternative themes that stand in tension with the selected

57 Matthew Kaemingk, *Christian Hospitality and Muslim Immigration in an Age of Fear* (Grand Rapids, MI: Eerdmans, 2018), esp. 147–52.

58 Kaemingk, 148.

focal image.[59] One focal image that Hays identifies is that of the cross, which is central to Paul's ethic, to the narratives of the gospel, to Revelation's ethical ideal of the martyr, and to other aspects of the New Testament. "Jesus' death on a cross is the paradigm for faithfulness to God in this world," Hays insists, clarifying, "The New Testament writers consistently employ the pattern of the cross precisely to call those who possess power and privilege to surrender it for the sake of the weak (see, e.g., Mark 10:42–45; Rom. 15:1–3; 1 Cor. 8:1–11:1)."[60] Hays renounces any use of the image of the cross to recklessly justify accepting abuse, but such an image necessarily includes a degree of risk. In the context of refugees, this means that we can expect to shoulder a degree of risk on behalf of the most vulnerable, except in extreme cases in which we exclude war criminals and enemy combatants under article 1F of the 1951 Refugee Convention.

To summarize, though the right to self-determination is an ethical good, in the context of refugee ethics, solidarity that is owed from general, special, or particular responsibility is a weightier moral consideration. When self-determination is used to exclude refugees, it often does so in the name of a false homogeneity that views refugees merely and often falsely as a threat, against common grace's insistence that they are a potential benefit too. It also shirks the risk of pain, acceptance of which for a good purpose is a central theme in New Testament ethics, an avoidance particularly egregious given the limited economic and national security risks posed by refugees.

---

59 Richard B. Hays, *The Moral Vision of the New Testament: A Contemporary Introduction to New Testament Ethics* (New York: Harper Collins, 1996), 189–90.

60 Hays, 197.

Appeal to the Goodness of Cultural Distinctions

Capitol Ministries publishes Bible studies for members of the US government, holding meetings for representatives, senators, and cabinet members to study the published lessons. In one lesson on immigration from 2019, Ralph Drollinger argues that "there must be national borders and boundaries," and "there must be enforcement of borders and boundaries."[61] Referencing the risk of terrorism and abuse of the welfare system,[62] exaggerated threats I have already addressed in chapter 5, Drollinger especially argues that God "frowns on illegal immigrants"[63] who have broken the law contrary to Romans 13:1–7. In contrast, God's scattering of peoples and diversification of languages in Genesis 11:6–8 reveals that "nations, by God's design, are to have different languages, cultures, and boundaries."[64] According to Drollinger, distinct nations, borders, and cultural variations are a good thing, but crossing borders without permission is a sin: "A bank robber, a murderer, and an illegal immigrant are all created in God's image, but that fact does not place them above the law of the land!"[65] This is the theology provided to many members of the US government, and at least some appear to accept it.

Drollinger's argument is different from the argument from self-determination already considered earlier. The argument from self-determination claims that the introduction of new cultures, religions, and ethical perspectives may constitute a harm

---

61 Ralph Drollinger, *What the Bible Says about Our Illegal Immigration Problem* (Phoenix, AZ: Capital Ministries, 2016), 5.

62 Drollinger, 1, 2, 8, 10.

63 Drollinger, 8.

64 Drollinger, 4. A similar argument is briefly presented in a more academic context in Zehnder, *Bible and Immigration*, 57–58.

65 Drollinger, *What the Bible Says*, 7.

to a society. Drollinger suggests that enforcing immigration law and maintaining borders is a positive good; presumably, even if unauthorized border crossings are made by individuals with a legitimate moral need, like asylees, the fact that they are acting contrary to these positive goods could be reason enough to exclude them. A similar argument is made by Markus Zehnder, who treats the distinction of ethnicities and nations as part of God's "creational order" evident in the "order and distinction" of God's creative work in Genesis 1. Mass immigration "disrupts order and undermines distinctions,"[66] while "God's creational intentions" are said to favor "specific ethnic groups living on specific territories defined by specific borders."[67] Maintaining the difference in people groups, with each maintaining its own state, is said to be the ideal.[68]

Drollinger's use of Scripture is not compelling, and he neglects the complexity of international law and domestic immigration policy, which expect undocumented border crossings as a means for refugees and asylees to secure the rights guaranteed them in the 1951 Refugee Convention. Scripturally, interpreting Romans 13 in isolation is problematic. Within Romans itself, Paul urges Christians to not be conformed to the world (12:1–2) and to not be conquered by evil (12:21).[69] Both commands might require civil disobedience if violence and nativist ideology is being used to promote death. There is a long biblical history

---

66 Zehnder, *Bible and Immigration*, 238. See also 60–61.
67 Zehnder, 239.
68 Zehnder thus charts the demographics of how mass immigration is leading to a decline in ethnic and religious homogeneity (167–82), arguing that such elimination of distinction undermines social cohesion (154–58, 266). A nation is said to have an "ethnic kernel," which can stand in tension with a more territorial definition of the nation (136–37). "The nation-state aspires at making the boundaries of state and nation congruent. This is, however, hardly fully achievable" (133).
69 Carroll R., *Bible and Borders*, 111–12; Choan-Seng Song, *Third-Eye Theology: Theology in Formation in Asian Settings* (Maryknoll, NY: Orbis, 1979), 211.

of civil disobedience, including Moses challenging Pharaoh's authority, which Paul references as God's plan in Romans 9:17.[70] In a broader canonical context, there are clear examples of civil disobedience undertaken to preserve life, including, notably, the Israelite midwives (Exod 1:15–21) and the magi who disobeyed Herod's command to share where the child was found (Matt 2:12), among others. Refugees and asylees who ignore a sovereign nation's refusal of entry for the purpose of preserving life are not clearly violating a moral good according to the biblical ethical vision.[71]

It is equally concerning that Drollinger focuses on Genesis 11 as a means of ensuring the separation of peoples, a similar exegetical strategy to one used in defense of segregation.[72] The intent of the story of the tower of Babel is more to reject those who disobey God's command to be fruitful and multiply, filling the earth (Gen 1:28), instead arrogantly trying to reach God. It is not about the inherent good of separating peoples. In fact, the New Testament offers a clear vision of the unity of peoples in Christ. Samuel Ngewa demonstrates the culturally unitive dimensions of pneumatology in Acts in his insightful analysis of the four instances where the charismatic gifts are given in a secondary event after conversion.[73] This occurs at Pentecost, where disciples who already believe in Christ receive the Holy

---

70 For a helpful balance of Rom 13 and Rom 9's reference to Moses, see Esau McCaulley, *Reading While Black: African American Biblical Interpretation as an Exercise in Hope* (Downers Grove, IL: InterVarsity Academic, 2020), 32.

71 I make this case more extensively in D. Glenn Butner Jr., "Undocumented Prudent Immigrants: De-centering Romans 13 and Rule of Law in Immigration Ethics," *Studies in Christian Ethics* 36, no. 1 (forthcoming).

72 J. Russell Hawkins, *The Bible Told Them So: How Southern Evangelicals Fought to Preserve White Supremacy* (Oxford: Oxford University Press, 2021), 49, 61–62.

73 See Samuel M. Ngewa, "Pneumatology: Its Implications for the African Context," in *The Spirit over the Earth: Pneumatology in the Majority World*, ed. Gene L. Green, Stephen T. Pardue, and K. K. Yeo (Grand Rapids, MI: Eerdmans, 2016), 99–121.

Spirit in dramatic fashion (Acts 2:2–4), again when Peter and John lay hands on Samaritan believers (Acts 8:17), a third time when Cornelius and his household received the Spirit (Acts 10:44–46), and a final time when Paul gives Ephesian Christians the baptism of the Holy Spirit (Acts 19:5–7). Ngewa claims that these instances are not signs of a regular second blessing in the Spirit but rather unique signs performed in front of apostles, "mark[ing] the uniting of other people groups into that body of believers established on the day of Pentecost," first Samaritans, then Gentiles, and finally peoples at the far ends of the known Empire.[74] Frank Thielman helpfully calls this aspect of Luke's theology "the triumph of inclusiveness" due to the continued expansion of the boundaries of the people of God despite resistance.[75] Through these charismatic gifts, God demonstrates that the new community of the faithful transcends any specific ethnos. When Markus Zehnder appeals to the creational order to argue for the good of distinct ethnic groups and nations, he dismisses appeals like those I mention here as "too vague to use them as concrete prescriptions for a particular policy."[76] However, the eschatological new creation community is a focal image of New Testament ethics, while his appeal to "creational orders" and ethnic distinction is virtually absent though equally vague in terms of policy prescription.[77]

As Kanan Kitani notes, "Like migrants, standing between two worlds, excluding neither but embracing both," Jesus incorporated many different groups. "Because he was at the margins, in his teaching and miracle-working, Jesus creates a new and

---

74 Ngewa, 117.

75 Frank Thielman, *Theology of the New Testament: A Canonical and Synthetic Approach* (Grand Rapids, MI: Zondervan, 2005), 127, 129.

76 Zehnder, *Bible and Immigration*, 246.

77 See Hays, *Moral Vision*, 198–200.

different center, the center constituted by the meeting of the borders of the many and diverse worlds, often in conflict with one another. . . . In Jesus, the margin where he lived became the center of a new society without borders and barriers, reconciling all peoples, 'Jew or Greek, slave or free, male or female' (Gal. 3:28)."[78] As I have already explored in dialogue with the work of Samuel Ngewa on Acts, the Holy Spirit's mission is also characterized by establishing a new community that transcends national and ethnic boundaries, even as the inaugurated eschatology of the New Testament requires us to continue to pay attention to things like nationality and ethnicity (as I have in this book). The Bible clearly teaches that in the new creation, there is an eschatological goal of the nations being united before their Creator (e.g., Is 66:18–20; Jer 3:16–17), and Israel regularly saw itself as calling the nations to begin to fulfill their eschatological purpose by coming to Israel to join in worshipping the true God today (see Pss 47, 96, and 117). As the church has been grafted into the promises of Israel, it has joined Israel's mission of drawing the nations to God (e.g., Matt 28:19; Luke 24:47). As peoples of various nations gather, it is in some sense a foretaste of the kingdom, even if the causes are evils that drive refugees from their homes.[79]

---

78 Kanan Kitani, "Jesus the Paradigmatic Migrant," in *Christian Theology in the Age of Migration: Implications for World Christianity*, ed. Peter C. Phan (Lanham, MD: Lexington, 2020), 140–41.

79 I do not intend by this theological claim to justify or excuse the evils that refugees may have experienced in their home countries, nor do I intend to explain why these evils have happened. It would be far too confident to believe that certain evils were permitted by God for the purpose of gathering the nations in this manner and too spiritually damaging to those who were wrestling with their pains to require them to accept *a priori* that God had acted for this purpose. In due course, some refugees may begin to see how their faith was enriched despite their experiences, and they may see benefits from their inclusion in new cross-cultural contexts, but such things are the lessons some refugees may learn through wisdom over time. For more on the risks of theodicy in the experiences of personal suffering, see John Swinton, *Raging with Compassion: Pastoral Responses to the Problem of Evil* (Grand Rapids, MI: Eerdmans, 2007).

Perhaps a more philosophical version of the argument will fare better. Nigel Biggar argues that community differences will naturally arise from distinct cultural boundaries, and Christians who trust in God's wisdom and sovereignty cannot treat any natural feature of creation as purely evil. In fact, different cultures and nations "enable human beings to learn from each other better ways of serving and promoting the human good."[80] In fact, according to Biggar, Christians have a unique reason to prefer segregated people groups given the diversity present within the Trinity (a complete misuse of the doctrine of the Trinity).[81] Therefore, we have a special duty to groups like our nation and our family to which we have a special tie. Because "borders exist primarily to define the territory within which a people is free to develop their own way of life," we must be leery of "unrestricted mobility" and prefer "negotiated" immigration.

It is clear to me that an increase in solidarity with refugees and asylees need not require a full-fledged cosmopolitanism that denies any borders. In fact, it is logically consistent to simultaneously argue (1) that borders and distinct countries are a moral good and (2) that refugee resettlement and asylum should be more frequently provided. Biggar himself accepts immigration on "certain conditions," though these remain underspecified.[82] In other words, it is possible to show solidarity with refugees while affirming the moral good of borders and of obedience to government.

---

80 Nigel Biggar, "The Value of Limited Loyalty: Christianity, the Nation, and Territorial Boundaries," in *Christian Political Ethics*, ed. James A. Coleman (Princeton, NJ: Princeton University Press, 2008), 96.
81 Biggar, 97.
82 Biggar, 102.

Our Duties to Refugees

If Jesus, Mary, and Joseph had fled persecution from Herod under the modern refugee system, it is tremendously unlikely that they would have received help. At the end of this chapter, I hope that this fact is recognized for what it is: a significant moral failing. All human beings have a general responsibility to care for all others, showing solidarity with them. For Christians, this solidarity is especially owed to refugees, who are among "the least of these" in solidarity with their Refugee King. Where questions arise regarding which refugees have the strongest claims on our protection, we can turn to the principles of restitution and relationship to identify those with whom we are especially obligated to show solidarity. In chapter 5, I already addressed potential utilitarian objections to my argument, showing that refugee-receiving nations are not worse off in terms of national security or the economy, such that economic and security interests do not justify our neglect of refugees. In this chapter, I have shown that competing ethical demands such as self-determination, cultural preservation, loyalty to one's country, or alternative conceptions of restitution do not eliminate our moral obligations to act in solidarity with refugees. Yet the concept of solidarity has remained at a theoretical level throughout my discussion. The time has come to specify what solidarity might look like in our current refugee regime, the subject of the seventh and final chapter.

7

Solidarity in Practice

THE PARABLE OF THE SHEEP and the goats calls us to solidarity
with refugees. But so far, my treatment of solidarity has been
largely theoretical. In this concluding chapter, I will provide specific steps through which Christians can show solidarity with
refugees. Ethicists and theologians have written many accounts
of solidarity, but I will be following a basic schema provided by
Kristen Heyer. According to Heyer, three dimensions of solidarity are "particularly well suited to addressing the challenges"
present in the modern international refugee regime.[1] Incarnational solidarity challenges Christians to be bodily present with
refugees; institutional solidarity requires the reform of laws,
policies, and institutions for the betterment of refugees; and

---

1 Heyer, *Kinship across Borders*, 114.

conflictual solidarity acknowledges that substantive and lasting change will require direct and vigorous challenges to forces that would oppose efforts to ensure that refugees' rights are protected. The duration of this chapter will involve connecting Heyer's three aspects of solidarity to the specific results of our thought experiment concerning whether the holy family would find protection in the modern refugee regime.

Incarnational Solidarity

A first practical step toward standing in solidarity with refugees is to help provide for their needs, including those of shelter, food, and clothing. As we have seen, such basic needs are often unmet, even within refugee camps. To name an example I have already mentioned, three thousand refugees inhabit the rat-infested Dunkirk refugee camp in France, where they live in tents and share access to two water taps for the entire community.[2] Several Christian nonprofits are involved in refugee resettlement and take donations and/or volunteers, including Church World Service, Episcopal Migration Ministries, Jesuit Refugee Service, Lutheran Immigration and Refugee Services, the United States Conference of Catholic Bishops, and World Relief. Additionally, since legal representation is so important for asylum seekers, donations to one of the countless organizations providing pro bono legal aid for asylum hearings would be of great benefit to asylees.

Providing financial and material support can be an aspect of solidarity, but on its own, it is merely charity. True solidarity is incarnational, requiring embodied community characterized by

---

2 Oliver, "Abolish Refugee Detention," 119.

mutuality and reciprocity. For this reason, Heyer characterizes such solidarity in terms of a humble presence and willingness to be transformed by refugees even as that presence is attempting to secure refugees' rights.[3] In similar terms, Juan Hernández Pico insists that solidarity occurs "only when believers advance toward a new alternative of personal and social life where equality prevails."[4] Solidarity exceeds aid because it includes reciprocity, and only in reciprocity is there genuine equality. Similarly, reciprocity is most realizable with embodied personal presence, not merely through financial donations from a distance through the anonymity of a nonprofit intermediary. In the Gospels' terms, such solidarity is embodied in welcoming the stranger, feeding the hungry, and clothing the naked (Matt 25:35–36), but it is also evident in the fact that those who need comfort and those who face poverty are considered blessed by Jesus (Matt 5:4; Luke 6:20). To put the matter in Pauline terminology, incarnational solidarity follows the example of Jesus, who became poor "so that by his poverty [we] might become rich" (2 Cor 8:9). Paul uses this model as a call to give to those in need (2 Cor 8:10–14) while teaching the Corinthians elsewhere that God has also chosen to build his church out of those of lowly estate (1 Cor 1:27–29).

Incarnational solidarity with refugees must establish a relationship of reciprocity, which challenges us to clarify what is meant by the very title of "refugee" and how those bearing the title of refugee are incorporated into various societies and cultures. Use of the title *refugee* may imply helplessness or may present refugees as mere victims.[5] Furthermore, the category of

---

3 Heyer, *Kinship across Borders*, 118.
4 Pico, "Solidarity with the Poor," 75.
5 See the discussion in Haddad, *Refugee in International Society*, 34–39.

refugee tends to ignore nationality, ethnicity, religion, and family history, leaving the refugee's need for safety or suffering under persecution as a central feature of the concept.[6] Citizens of host countries that deny refugees and asylees the right to work or to participate in educational and political processes may also be led to objectify refugees. Under such circumstances, refugees may appear to be victims simply because they are denied the opportunity to use their gifts and abilities, leaving such abilities unrecognized and unappreciated.[7] Some refugees voice frustration at the dehumanizing dimension of being reduced to a refugee with unrecognized abilities and personal identities. For example, refugees who reach Melilla, the Spanish city in Morocco, are typically housed for extended periods in a detention center as they are processed and considered for asylum in Europe. One refugee describes the situation as follows: "They see refugees, not human beings."[8]

Luke Bretherton explores the way that humanitarianism as an ideology can reinforce the marginalization of those benefiting from humanitarian efforts, which would include many refugees receiving nongovernmental organization (NGO) assistance. Such NGOs are often in a "triage situation," unable to adequately consider needed political and institutional changes, ultimately undermining the ability of recipients of humanitarian aid to self-govern, as many NGOs by design or default play a significant role in the governance of the communities they

---

6 Michel Agier, *On the Margins of the World: The Refugee Experience Today*, trans. David Fernbach (Cambridge: Polity, 2008), 49; Alexander Betts and Paul Collier, *Refuge: Rethinking Refugee Policy in a Changing World* (Oxford: Oxford University Press, 2017), 158.

7 Owen, *What Do We Owe*, 78.

8 Vella, *Dying to Live*, 73.

support.[9] In fact, as various NGOs and even the United Nations High Commissioner for Refugees (UNHCR) take increasing leadership in managing the refugee resettlement and/or asylum hearing process, these organizations themselves can become responsible through their governance for human rights violations such as denials of due process; inadequate provision of basic shelter, food, and clothing; and failure to provide basic security.[10] Bretherton adds that the need to fundraise creates an ongoing temptation to "play off racialized, demeaning, and infantilizing stereotypes" because such tropes can generate larger revenue streams.[11] When situated within a culture of philanthropy that emphasizes the wealth and kindness of donors, humanitarianism can emphasize the distance between those who provide care and those who receive it.[12] Far better, Bretherton argues, to repent in the face of the moral problem of poverty than to elevate oneself as the solution to that problem.[13] To this I would add that it is equally important to recognize and affirm the capabilities of refugees beyond, refusing to view them as merely victims.

Jesus, God's beloved Son and Savior of the world, would have had to pass through the international refugee system if he fled to Egypt today rather than in the first century. This is a fact that reminds us of a truth where we should need no reminding—displaced persons are capable of amazing things. Refugees are not merely victims but often display great courage and perseverance in crossing borders while showing considerable initiative to find work and a place to live.[14] When given the

---

9 Luke Bretherton, *Christ and the Common Life: Political Theology and the Case for Democracy* (Grand Rapids, MI: Eerdmans, 2019), 56–58.

10 See the extensive examples provided in Verdirame and Harrell-Bond, *Rights in Exile*.

11 Bretherton, *Christ and the Common Life*, 58.

12 Bretherton, 67.

13 Bretherton, 68.

14 The point is well made in De La Torre, *Trails of Hope*, 145.

chance to work, refugees frequently display a remarkable ability to impact the cultures in which they settle. For example, in Catania, Italy, refugees Lucien and Abdel founded Africa Unita, an organization that cares for refugees as they arrive in Europe. Lucien claims he founded the organization "to show that refugees and migrants can do more than people think."[15] Similarly, Amalia and Gil were Salvadorans who fled violence but were put in detention while pursuing asylum after overstaying their visas. While in detention, Amalia understood her role to be "helping the other prisoners overcome their fear, strengthen their faith, and find God's love in this place." She led Bible studies and served as an informal translator between guards and detainees. She and Gil also made trinkets in prison, which they were able to sell for about $50 a week, just enough to help their kids buy beans and rice to eat while their eldest child worked to pay rent. Amalia even wrote the courts a letter on behalf of a detainee that did not speak English, securing a court date that eventually led to the woman being reunited with her children.[16] Such stories remind us of the ingenuity of asylees and refugees.

Of course, it is easy to compile a few heartwarming stories, just as I could also find a few terrifying stories of migrants who have committed atrocious crimes to drive the reader to fear refugees. Anecdotal stories can manipulate—the example of criminal immigrants may mislead by suggesting higher crime rates among immigrants, despite considerable evidence to the contrary. Similarly, a few stories of productive refugees could theoretically mask the fact that they are a larger burden on society.

---

15 Vella, *Dying to Live*, 155.
16 Matthew Colwell, "Proclaiming Liberty to the Captives: Amalia Molina," in *Our God Is Undocumented: Biblical Faith and Immigrant Justice*, ed. Ched Myers and Matthew Colwell (Maryknoll, NY: Orbis, 2012), 115–16.

But close examination of the evidence reveals that this is not the case; providing refugees with economic opportunities can be a great benefit to the host nation. However, I must admit that we cannot shoehorn any group of people into monolithic categories. Not every refugee is an entrepreneur; many others will simply be quality employees and laborers. As is the case among any people group, refugee groups will also have elderly members, caregivers, and children who cannot be expected to work. Despite this, there are larger case studies that show the ingenuity and economic productivity of refugees.

Uganda has especially proven the ingenuity of refugees through its "Self-Reliance strategy," which allows refugees from neighboring nations access to land, work, and free movement while refusing the use of camps except in rare circumstances.[17] Refugees have farmed and developed restaurants, shops, wholesalers, importers, and recreational ventures, like a man named Abdi's video game studio where refugees can come play old PlayStation consoles.[18] Alexander Betts and Paul Collier summarize, "In Kampala 21 per cent of refugees run a business that creates jobs, and, of their employees, 40 per cent are citizens of the host country."[19] In other words, refugees are creating jobs for Ugandan citizens. Refugees in Uganda have also been able to provide for their economic needs. The average annual household income is $468 per year, though some refugees reached as high as $1,800 per year.[20] These numbers are low, but the average household income in Uganda is only $1,392, according to a 2016/17 survey

---

17 Betts and Collier, *Refuge*, 160.
18 Betts and Collier, 162–63.
19 Betts and Collier, 165.
20 Betts and Collier, 163.

of the Uganda Bureau of Statistics.[21] This means that many refugee households have been able to generate employment, and some have even reached a level above the average household income in Uganda. This is not to suggest that the Self-Reliance strategy has been perfect. Refugees still face discrimination by Ugandan citizens, and they often receive inferior-quality land plots.[22] However, granting these shortcomings, it is certainly the case that refugees in Uganda are in a better situation than those who are left in camps with no annual household income, no access to employment and land, and little opportunity for resettlement. They are also in a better situation than those refugees who settle in urban areas as undocumented immigrants, lacking legal access to economic opportunities. No doubt many refugees would be content with local integration instead of resettlement, provided that they were granted opportunities to work.

Given the evidence of the economic ingenuity and hard work of many refugees, one specific way to show incarnational solidarity to refugees and asylees is to provide them with employment opportunities. Partly, this will be a matter of personal decisions, as human resources representatives, management, and/or owners of small businesses make employment choices. However, labor laws are also a factor. Restrictive laws may prohibit hiring refugees, or administrative hurdles might make such hiring challenging to the point that some firms are unwilling to bother. The experience of refugees in Ugandan communities is sadly not the norm, as many countries do not allow those in camps to seek employment. Other refugees who fit the legal requirements

---

21 Uganda Bureau of Statistics, *Uganda National Household Survey 2016/2017 Report* (Kampala: Uganda Bureau of Statistics, 2017), accessed October 25, 2021, https://www.ubos.org/wp-content/uploads/publications/03_20182016_UNHS_FINAL_REPORT.pdf, 109.

22 Betts and Collier, *Refuge*, 161.

of protection but recognize the immense challenges of passing through the asylum process choose instead to live in urban areas as undocumented immigrants, which results in further inability to access labor markets. Such factors point to the fact that incarnational solidarity must be coupled with institutional solidarity to be effective.

Institutional Solidarity

Given the systemic injustices in the international refugee regime, it is impossible to exemplify solidarity with refugees without evaluating and changing institutions. Solidarity requires taking responsibility, and in the context of refugee ethics, "a commitment to solidarity calls nations to understand themselves as collectively responsible for the international order," explains Heyer.[23] If we consider the conduct of many nations, they simply have not taken responsibility for securing the rights of refugees, and this failure demands a change in institutional priorities. As Mark and Luke Glanville note, "Many of these Western states expend significantly more resources keeping displaced people at a distance than they do contributing to international efforts to care for them."[24] I would add that many Western nations also spend more on military intervention that creates refugees than they do on care for refugees. For example, in 2007, the United States supplied $20 million to the UNHCR for Iraqi refugees (one-third of the total needed) while spending $2 billion a week on the war.[25] That same year, US Immigration and Customs Enforcement (ICE) spent $12 million just to detain two

---

23 Heyer, *Kinship across Borders*, 114.
24 Glanville and Glanville, *Refuge Reimagined*, 203.
25 García, *Refugee Challenge*, 113.

thousand refugees in one facility in Pearsall, Texas.[26] A 2008 immigration enforcement raid of Agriprocessors, Inc. (the largest federal raid in history at the time) cost $5.2 million, or "$13,396 for each of the 389 undocumented workers taken into custody."[27] Admittedly, the United States is in the complex situation of having often led the world in refugee resettlement while also being a leader in many military operations that help create refugee crises in the first place. I do not intend to deny the good that Americans have done, but neither can we ignore the harmful effects of US policies and institutions.

Critique should not be limited to the United States. Only twenty-nine countries provided refugee resettlement in 2019,[28] meaning that most of the world's countries simply did not show solidarity to refugees. If states are unwilling to share the responsibility of hosting the refugee, then the state where the refugee applied for protection is expected to provide it and is prohibited from refoulement. This incentivizes states where asylees might first seek protection to try to limit applicants through the violence and denials of due process discussed earlier in this work.[29] As we saw in chapter 4, the European Union has militarized its borders and made every effort to intercept and turn back potential refugees and asylees before they reach European soil. Many European nations, too, have prioritized spending on security over solidarity.

---

26 Kendall, *From Gulag to Guantanamo*, 95.

27 De La Torre, *Trails of Hope*, 88.

28 Glanville and Glanville, *Refuge Reimagined*, 221. The refugee resettlement situation has grown far more complicated since the outbreak of Covid-19.

29 Owen, "Refugees and the Politics," 17–18.

Systemic Injustice and Institutional Solidarity

When I consider the international refugee regime, I interpret it as an example of systemic injustice. By this, I intentionally allude to two possible meanings of the word *systemic*. First, I mean that the injustice is structural, involving a convergence of laws and policies, institutions, and the beliefs and actions of individuals. As we considered the holy family's circumstances under the hypothetical scenario of their pursuit of asylum under the 1951 Refugee Convention, we saw a broad range of barriers to their protection. Jesus likely would not find protection because of unjust policies, such as Operation Streamline, which would likely deny due process and the chance to have a real asylum hearing. Yet we can ask the question, Why are policies like Operation Streamline in place? Certainly, some support exclusionary policies because of their nativism or racism. For example, when the United States welcomed Vietnamese refugees at the end of the Vietnam War, Congressperson Burt Talcott fought the resettlement, saying, "Damn it, we have too many Orientals."[30] Sometimes the prejudice is more subtle. As I explored in chapter 5, many hold the false belief that immigrants are a security threat, which also prompts voters to support political candidates who will be hard on immigration. Prejudiced ideas lead to unjust laws passed by politicians who campaigned on the promise of policies just like Operation Streamline. Yet though prejudice is certainly a factor in policies like Operation Streamline, unjust denial of due process is not exclusively a result of prejudiced opinions, and not everyone who is involved with policies like

---

30 Jenna M. Loyd and Alison Mountz, *Boats, Borders, and Bases: Race, the Cold War, and the Rise of Migration Detention in the United States* (Oakland: University of California Press, 2018), 40.

Operation Streamline harbors anti-immigrant sentiments. Systemic problems are more expansive than the sinful thoughts and beliefs of individuals.

The lack of due process in Operation Streamline can also be traced to a lack of resources and a lack of information by some voters. Once a zero-tolerance policy is set for immigration violations, there is an immediate increase in caseloads, which often simply cannot be handled within existing court structures. There just are not enough trained attorneys, judges, and courthouses to facilitate every hearing, so hearings en masse are the inevitable result.[31] In principle, with a greater allocation of resources, a zero-tolerance policy toward immigration violations would not need to lead to a loss of due process for potential asylees (though it may still be objectionable on other grounds). Other voters are likely unaware of the existence of Operation Streamline while voting on the basis of other political issues for candidates who will support (or at least fail to end) practices like Operation Streamline. The continued denial of due process through Operation Streamline would not be possible without the lack of budget and voter awareness.

So far, I have considered how a combination of prejudice, budgetary limitations, and lack of awareness leads to the existence of a policy like Operation Streamline with its denial of due process. Individuals and groups who are not directly involved in the day-to-day operations of Operation Streamline are the cause of many of these factors, but part of the injustice in Operation

---

31 Lydgate, "Assembly-Line Justice," 9. Lydgate notes that the extreme workload also leads to burnout, causing employee-retention problems, furthering the shortage of qualified prosecution and defense attorneys. Other observers may not be convinced about this explanation, since Border Patrol apprehends far more migrants each day than they can even process through Operation Streamline, such that many are simply returned across the border. Zero-tolerance policies are often not fully enforced. Thompson, *Border Odyssey*, 224.

Streamline comes from those who work within the legal and detention processes associated with the policy. For example, recent internal reports from the US Department of Homeland Security obtained under the Freedom of Information Act narrate incidents where detainees were denied food until they signed papers in English that they could not understand or where a detainee injured by a Customs and Border Patrol dog was denied medical care for the injury for over a month while in custody. The same report narrates the use of racist language, threats, and violence against detainees.[32] Such incidents of malice are clearly immoral, and the US immigration system would be greatly improved if such incidents stopped immediately. However, a full institutional correction for Operation Streamline will require deeper changes. The unjust laws and policies explored in this work, like Operation Streamline, are a complex by-product of prejudice, malice, lack of awareness, budgetary limitations, and unanticipated outcomes of bureaucratic policies. Reform would require changes at the level of individual beliefs and actions, policies and laws, and budgetary decisions.

The second thing I intend to point out in speaking of systemic justice in the international refugee regime is that the injustice is pervasive, present throughout various institutional levels. We cannot dismiss these injustices as merely the result of a few bad apples. Many refugees and asylees face a denial of due process despite being eligible for refugee status under international law, EU law, and US law. Operation Streamline, a complex result of prejudice, budgetary limits, malice, and lack of awareness by

---

32 Clara Long et al., *They Treat You like You Are Worthless: Internal DHS Reports of Abuse by US Border Officials* (New York: Human Rights Watch, 2021), 1–3, 13–25, accessed October 22, 2021, https://www.hrw.org/sites/default/files/media_2021/10/us _borderabuses1021_web.pdf.

voters, is one instance of such a lack of due process, but it is not the only one. Efforts to deny hearings to refugees and asylees are pervasive throughout the US immigration system, from the superficial and sporadic screenings for asylum eligibility held for migrants who are intercepted by the Coast Guard in the Gulf of Mexico, to the denial of any possibility of an asylum hearing at most US embassies, to restrictions that prevent possible asylees from flying into the United States to claim asylum, to the practice of leaving the vast majority of refugees in camps for years on end without seriously considering them for resettlement. Cumulatively, these instances involve domestic immigration policy, international law, the policies and practices of companies like airlines that make travel restrictions possible, and many citizens who vote for candidates running on a platform that centers on restricting immigration. Fixing the situation would require an extensive overhaul of current practice, not merely the replacement of a few key personnel.

How do we think about who is culpable for the systemic injustice found in the international refugee system? After all, to speak of systemic injustice is to suggest that someone is guilty. I do not intend to write a full analysis exploring the distribution of guilt among those responsible for the plight of many modern refugees. It is far more important to me to outline who has a responsibility to work to change the current situation. Nevertheless, I would like to offer a few preliminary reflections on the question of culpability. Obviously, some will be guilty in a straightforward manner, such as those who undertake acts of violence against refugees or those who advocate or circulate racist or nativist ideas about immigrants. Others are complicit with the injustice in a less direct manner. Such complicity may stem from not doing the good one knows ought to be done (Jas 4:17; Prov

3:27), failing to take a good action. Complicity may also relate to failing to prevent an evil that is within one's power to prevent (e.g., Exod 21:29).[33] Such complicity follows from inaction, but complicity may also arise from indirect participation in practices that are not just. Following traditional distinctions made by many moral theologians, we can also distinguish between material and formal complicity with evil. Material complicity does not require consent, as when the taxpayers' money is used to prevent due process for refugees, but a taxpayer is unaware of these practices or objects to them. Formal complicity occurs when consent is present. One who does not directly use violence against refugees but who knows of such violence and supports it by voting for candidates who promise to use such violence is formally complicit. Formal complicity involves guilt, while material complicity may suggest a responsibility to correct the injustice without implying guilt.[34]

As explained in chapter 4, one reason why so many refugees remain in camps without having genuine opportunities for resettlement is that countries do not take responsibility for resettlement. Most of the world's countries have signed onto the 1951 Refugee Convention or the 1967 Protocol, acknowledging that refugees ought to have resettlement opportunities and rights, but individual nations do not see a duty to provide for these rights and resettlement. As Serena Parekh notes, countries are exercising their legitimate ability to determine who can

---

33 In the case of the unrestrained ox in Exod 21, the owner has the knowledge and ability to prevent an evil but has not done so. This is evaluated by the law as a distinct level of moral responsibility. The murderer faces the death penalty (Exod 21:12), while the one who fails to take action to prevent a preventable death of another may simply pay a financial restitution (Exod 21:30).

34 See the treatment in Daniel C. McGuire, "Cooperation with Evil," in *The Westminster Dictionary of Christian Ethics*, ed. James F. Childress and John Macquarrie (Philadelphia: Westminster John Knox, 1986), 129.

enter their territory, but the problem is one of coordinated (in)action.[35] When all countries are too restrictive, the rights of refugees are not secured. Therefore, identifying the countries that directly bear responsibility for specific refugee groups helps us move beyond abstract notions of solidarity to specific demands of justice. The principles of restitution and relationship discussed in chapter 6 help identify such responsibilities.

Public Policy and Institutional Solidarity

So far, my discussion of institutional solidarity has focused on the ethical dimensions of such solidarity. Full institutional solidarity will, of course, require specific reforms to specific institutions. A full reform package would require extensive input from lawyers, economists, political scientists, and sociologists in addition to insights from ethicists like me. However, the process of imagining Jesus, Mary, and Joseph passing through our modern refugee system has revealed several specific institutional reforms that the average reader can advocate for easily and immediately through direct communication with their representatives in government. I will offer six urgent policy reforms.

First, chapter 4 explored the widespread denial of due process to refugees evident in Operation Streamline, in the interception of refugees in the Mediterranean and Caribbean, and in the refusal to process asylum applications in locations to which refugees can reasonably have access. Any solidarity with refugees

---

35 Parekh, *No Refuge*, 165–67. Parekh does not focus on how guilt produces responsibility. "I am not responsible because I am *guilty*," Parekh explains, but because "[I] participate in diverse institutional processes that produce injustice" (169). I will focus more on guilt leading to responsibility and duty when I discuss restitution. However, the relational basis of duty that I will discuss fits more with Parekh's notion of responsibility.

will require that mass hearings like Operation Streamline end immediately and that due process be granted to potential asylees. Despite my attempt to deflate the alleged security risks posed by refugees, some may prioritize the need to secure national borders against undocumented asylees. Such individuals can still advocate that due process be provided in offshore processing facilities, or at foreign embassies. Ideally, neutral observers could ensure that due process is being provided.

The second and third reforms are closely related. Governments have the authority to determine which groups and how many within such groups are admitted through immigration processes. A second urgent institutional change is the immediate increase of refugee ceilings in most European and North American countries.[36] As discussed in chapter 4, most encamped refugees wait years for resettlement opportunities that never arrive. Increased levels of refugee admission will improve this situation. It is important to increase not only permissible levels of refugee admissions but actual admitted refugees. In the United States, the Biden administration, for example, set an admission ceiling of 62,500 for the 2021 fiscal year, far short of historic American admissions. However, just 11,411 refugees were welcomed into the United States, a record low.[37] A third urgent reform relates to nonconvention refugees, a subject discussed in chapter 2. The 1951 Refugee Convention restricts the definition to those with a reasonable fear of persecution for a relevant category who are

---

36 These regions are the focus of this study, but there is certainly room for improvement in countries that fall outside of these regions. Since I have not discussed such areas in any detail, I will not discuss here where such areas can improve.

37 This is the official number reported by the Refugee Processing Center, the division of the US Department of State charged with tracking resettlement, among many other responsibilities. For continually updated numbers each month, see Department of State, *PRM Admissions Report*, Refugee Processing Center, June 2022, https://www.wrapsnet.org/admissions-and-arrivals/.

unable to find assistance from their government. Individuals fleeing from war or environmental disasters, for example, are not eligible according to this legal definition, which is incorporated into law in many states that have endorsed the 1951 convention. Because individuals persecuted by their own governments are particularly vulnerable, a case can be made for the validity of this restrictive definition as a means of prioritizing care for the most vulnerable.[38] This does not, however, eliminate the responsibility to show solidarity with nonconvention refugees. Many countries attempt to fulfill this responsibility through the provision of other protected statuses. The United States, for example, relies on Temporary Protected Status (TPS) for nonconvention refugees displaced by natural disasters. However, TPS is problematic in several regards. First, immigration opportunities like TPS are most often granted to groups who already have vocal representation within the United States. Second, though TPS was designed for periods of up to eighteen months without a path to citizenship, Congress has repeatedly extended this time frame for specific groups as the economic fallout of disasters drags on. This leaves many families in situations of uncertainty, as they have no path to citizenship, no certainty about their current residential status, and no reasonable ability to return home.[39] For this

---

38 See Kristin Walker, "Defending the 1951 Convention Definition of Refugee," *Georgetown Immigration Law Journal* 17, no. 4 (2003): 583–609. Walker views the 1951 definition as a compromise between state sovereignty and international protection of human rights, and a good one at that. Those persecuted by their home countries are in a different condition than those fleeing natural disasters, for example, and require a different sort of care, including access to a new society where their fundamental rights will not be denied. Many facing poverty, war, or natural disaster can be helped in their home context and need not receive asylum. Walker's argument does not adequately consider the situation of failed states with long-standing violence, which may functionally deny the rights of residents within failed states. Despite this, her main points have moral plausibility to them.

39 For a helpful summary of the issues, see Dakin-Grimm, *Dignity and Justice*, 145–46, 174–76.

reason, an important third institutional reform is to advocate that provisions be made for nonconvention refugees in a manner that provides long-term stability, including a path to citizenship.

Once asylees enter a country, one major barrier is the significant backlog in asylum cases. In 2017, the journal of the American Bar Association reported that there was a backlog of over 540,000 asylum cases, and some judges were setting hearing dates for six years in the future.[40] A fourth and fifth practical institutional reform arise from this backlog. Increased funding and staffing for immigration courts could ensure that hearings were more efficient and effective, so a fourth institutional reform calls for increased personnel in immigration courts. Asylum applicants who must wait a decade may be prohibited from working legally during this time. Clearly, it is not possible for an asylee to live without income for such a long time, which means many are faced with the choice of working without legal permission or relying on social welfare support, neither of which is ideal for the asylee or for the American economy. As I write this, unemployment is at record-low rates in the United States, with many retail, food service, and manual labor jobs going unfilled. The provision of work opportunities, a fifth reform, can benefit all concerned parties.

A sixth important action step that readers can immediately pursue is to resist foreign policy that might contribute to the creation of refugees, either directly through foreign military intervention or indirectly through the support of governments that persecute their citizens. I have noted in this work how the United States has funded or provided military equipment or

---

40 Lorelei Laird, "Legal Logjam: Neglect and Political Interference Have Created a Growing Backlog in Immigration Courts of 540,000-plus Cases," *ABA Journal* 103, no. 4 (April 2017): 54.

training to various governments or military groups in El Salvador, Haiti, and Nicaragua that produced refugees through widespread human rights violations. Many more examples could be added to this list. The electorate can work to hold politicians accountable for supporting totalitarian regimes. Similarly, military action reliably produces nonconvention refugees and internally displaced persons, but if recent results of American wars are any indication, military intervention is unreliable in producing desired foreign policy outcomes. Again, political resistance to military action abroad can be an important step toward preventing refugees. Where wars are unavoidable, a concerted effort must be made to protect noncombatants, which will include providing for asylees and refugees.[41]

While much more institutional reform is surely needed to correct the failings of the international refugee regime, these six specific suggestions can result in substantial improvement, and many of these actions can be taken relatively quickly. Unless these and further changes are made, the current refugee regime will continue to be marred by systemic injustice.

Conflictual Solidarity

While solidarity is incarnational and institutional, Heyer also reminds us that it is often conflictual: "The solidarity demanded amid the chasm wreaked by unjust forms of globalization necessarily entails conflict."[42] Incarnational solidarity alone may be insufficient, even when expressed in the biblically warranted

---

41 Indeed, noncombatant immunity is a centerpiece of just war theory, whether in Christian or secular form. See Daniel M. Bell Jr., *Just War as Christian Discipleship: Recentering the Tradition in the Church Rather Than the State* (Grand Rapids, MI: Brazos, 2009), 209–36.

42 Heyer, *Kinship across Borders*, 119.

form of hospitality—welcoming the stranger. Often, without conflict, there can be no progress. Heyer argues that some of those who benefit from systems of injustice are unlikely to foster the necessary level of reform without pressure, while others will be unaware of the urgent moral issues refugees face if they are not confronted with them directly.[43] In Heyer's words, "In a world where luxury and misery rub shoulders, economic idolatry serves to avert our gaze from Lazarus."[44] Conflictual solidarity, on the other hand, can force one to gaze upon Lazarus, or, to use the framework of this book, it can compel us to gaze upon the refugee in whom Christ is found today. What does conflictual solidarity look like in terms of the international refugee regime?

In 2016, a poll found that most residents in the European Union believe that refugees increased the likelihood of terrorism, and nearly a third believed that refugees were responsible for more crimes than other groups.[45] Ernesto Castañeda and Casey Chiappetta contrast claims by politicians and law enforcement that the southern US border is not safe with a survey of residents of various neighborhoods in El Paso, a border city. The results of the survey were that 3.1 percent of residents claimed their neighborhood was not safe, while 96.9 percent claimed that their neighborhood was safe or very safe.[46] As discussed in chapter 5, the fear of refugees and asylees as a terrorist or criminal threat runs contrary to numerous empirical studies. One study found that the biggest predictor of whether someone would perceive refugees as a terrorist threat was not the actual presence or absence of terrorist acts, nor was it the number of terrorists arrested in that

---

43 Heyer, 120–21.
44 Heyer, 121.
45 Wike, Stokes, and Simmons, "Wave of Refugees," 3.
46 Ernesto Castañeda and Casey Chiappetta, "Border Residents' Perceptions of Crime and Security in El Paso, Texas," *Social Sciences* 9, no. 3 (2020): 24–39.

individual's country. Instead, the best predictor was political affiliation.[47] This suggests that much of the fear directed toward immigrants in general and refugees in particular is based on ideology rather than data. Given this fact, one practical means of practicing the conflictual dimension of solidarity is to challenge those in your circles of influence who describe refugees and asylees as a threat to national or personal security. Challenging these perceptions may not be easy and often will result in conflict, but without a change in the perceptions of a substantial number of Americans and Europeans, it is unlikely that the current refugee regime will see significant changes.

Conflictual solidarity may also be demonstrated through preaching. Certainly, preaching on immigration will not be the centerpiece of most pulpits, for good reason. The pastor is called to preach the whole counsel of God with special emphasis on the good news of the salvation provided by Jesus Christ, the central theme of the Bible. However, since there is extensive biblical content on immigration, including subjects relevant to the situation of refugees, a pastor committed to preaching the whole counsel of God will necessarily also need to preach about immigration on occasion. Preaching is also contextualized to the particular situation of the congregation.[48] In communities where nativism or racism are prevalent, preaching may adopt a more conflictual posture; in congregations that contain many immigrants,

---

47 Bartłomiej Walczak and Nikolaos Lampas, "Beliefs on Refugees as a Terrorist Threat: The Social Determinants of Refugee-Related Stereotypes," *Studia Migracyjne Przegląd Polonijny* 176, no. 2 (2020): 53–70.

48 I particularly appreciate the image developed by James Cleland and deployed by William Clair Turner Jr. of preaching as an ellipse, whose circumference is determined by two foci: the biblical text and the preacher's context. See William Clair Turner Jr., *Preaching That Makes the Word Plain: Doing Theology in the Crucible of Life* (Eugene, OR: Cascade, 2008), 4. The best text I am familiar with that explores the significance of context for preaching is Matthew D. Kim, *Preaching with Cultural Intelligence: Understanding the People Who Hear Our Sermons* (Grand Rapids, MI: Baker Academic, 2017).

more sermons will need to address the range of experiences immigrants, including refugees, may face. While institutional reform is necessarily the domain of government, only the church is charged with preaching the Scriptures to bring about both saving conversion and subsequent moral conversions.

Let me illustrate with an example: I had the privilege of participating in a diversity initiative at Sterling College where I teach in the Theology and Ministry Department. Part of the initiative involved interviewing students individually or in small groups to listen to their experiences at our institution and in the community in Sterling, Kansas. We soon saw two themes: first, students of all races regularly spoke of the hospitality and kindness shown to them on campus and in the community. Most Sterling residents are truly remarkable in their generosity and welcome. However, we also began to hear consistent stories of anti-Hispanic bigotry, where students were told to "go back to Mexico" (regardless of their country of origin), were accosted for speaking Spanish, or were confronted in a bar in a nearby town. In fact, I did not interview a single Latina student who had not been the victim of such racist bigotry in some way in Sterling, and many also had stories from their home communities too. Roughly half of the Latina students interviewed were immigrants, so the issues of the virtues of hospitality to immigrants and the sin of racism converged in these interviews. In this context, I found it important to address this widespread pattern from the pulpits of several churches where I occasionally am invited to preach. These sermons on texts like Luke 10:25–27, Acts 10:23b–48, and Exodus 22:21 were more conflictual than many I preach, but they addressed a sin in the community of Sterling with specific biblical principles with a call to action. I recognize that there is nothing heroic about guest preachers touching on such subjects when their jobs are not on the line as some local pastors' might be. Yet I hope this illustrates the kinds of situations where conflictual preaching on subjects related to immigration is necessary.

A third conflictual dimension of solidarity with Jesus the Refugee is political action. Political action is not simplistic partisanship. In the American context, I have mentioned the ethical failings of the immigration policies of the presidential administrations of Jimmy Carter, Ronald Reagan, George H. W. Bush, Bill Clinton, George W. Bush, Barack Obama, Donald Trump, and Joe Biden. Though the United States has led the way in refugee resettlement and provides extensive funding to the UNHCR, presidential administrations from both parties have favored foreign policies that create refugees through international military action while supporting policies that restrict care for refugees through the militarization of borders and denial of due process to asylees and refugees. This does not mean that all administrations are equally problematic in terms of refugee care—I find the Trump administration's policies of child separation, for example, to be particularly morally egregious. It does mean that Christians can expect there to be policies of any American presidential administration in the near future that must be challenged through political action, be it through voting, petitions, protests, or contributing financially to lobbying organizations.

My appeal to the need to engage in politics through the state will not be convincing to all. One might argue, as Daniel Bell does against liberation theology (which influences my account of solidarity),[49] that the church is better off to avoid "politics

---

49 This is evident in my appeal to John Sobrino and Juan Hernández Pico in defining solidarity or my reliance at several key points on the analysis of Miguel De La Torre or the general trend of a Christology of solidarity—Christ the refugee mirrors in certain respects Sobrino's Christ the victim, for example.

as statecraft," instead recognizing that the church itself can be a political entity.[50] Bell explains that politics as statecraft emerges partly from the prevalent post–Vatican II sense that grace pervades everything such that all things have a supernatural finality. In other words, "it is precisely because the world is already infused with grace that liberationists feel free to maintain the autonomy of the political realm."[51] Capitalism is the primary target of liberationist critique, but Bell argues that the state cannot resist capitalism because true resistance would require the reformation of desire, something properly the domain of the church.

Bell is correct to point toward the need for ecclesiology to maintain a political dimension, and he is right that the transformation of desire is the proper domain of the church. Any statecraft-based attempt to transform the culture that views the refugee as a threat rather than as an opportunity to show solidarity with Christ is doomed to fail.[52] It is also the case that the church is capable of further political acts beyond those focusing on desire. In the United States, one thinks of the controversial sanctuary movement, which began in the 1980s, where local congregations provided protection and housing for undocumented Latin American asylum seekers who were displaced in part by American interventionism and who therefore were

---

50 Daniel M. Bell Jr., *Liberation Theology after the End of History: The Refusal to Cease Suffering* (New York: Routledge, 2001), 65–73.

51 Bell, 63.

52 For a more detailed account of the all-too-common failed attempt to change culture through politics as statecraft, see James Davison Hunter, *To Change the World: The Irony, Tragedy, and Possibility of Christianity in the Late Modern World* (Oxford: Oxford University Press, 2010).

unlikely to receive asylum for political reasons.[53] In Europe, the Bethel Church in the Netherlands provides a similar example of a church showing conflictual solidarity with refugees. The Dutch government was poised to deport the Tamrazyan family after a failed asylum application, despite their insistence that they would not be safe in Armenia, their home, due to the political activism of the father, Sasun Tamrazyan. Taking advantage of a medieval law still on the books that prohibits authorities from interrupting a worship service, Bethel Church held a ninety-six-day-long worship service with hundreds of congregants and pastors volunteering in shifts to hold the service, all while the Tamrazyans lived in the church building. After ninety-six days and international media attention, the government agreed to modify its asylum policy and permit the Tamrazyan family, and dozens of other families, to remain in the Netherlands.[54] Local churches can play a role in conflictual solidarity.

It is nevertheless a pragmatic necessity that political efforts include statecraft. Issues like the militarization of borders, justice in the courtroom, and legal permission for asylees to work

---

53 A brief narrative summary of the sanctuary movement is found in De La Torre, *Immigration Crisis*, 109–32. For criticism of the use of Old Testament sanctuary cities as a basis for the modern sanctuary movement, see Zehnder, *Bible and Immigration*, 16–17. For all of Zehnder's concern about misuse and misapplication of the Bible, his objections neglect the issues of the application of Scripture. To put it simply, what was historically called the moral sense of Scripture and today goes by names like "the rule of purpose" is completely neglected in his treatment of sanctuary. This is problematic, since the entire question concerns whether the basic moral principles underlying ancient protections for manslaughterers might be contextualized today in defense of asylum seekers. While there is certainly no exact correlation, it is at least the case that both applications of the sanctuary concept concern the protection of individuals who may face unjust harm under their native civic law and customs. On the rule of purpose, see Charles Cosgrove, *Appealing to Scripture in Moral Debate: Five Hermeneutical Rules* (Grand Rapids, MI: Eerdmans, 2002), 12–50.

54 Andy Gregory, "Family Shielded from Deportation in Dutch Church for Three Months Finally Granted Asylum," *Independent*, January 31, 2019, accessed December 31, 2021, https://www.independent.co.uk/news/world/dutch-church-family-deportation -granted-asylum-tamrazyan-netherlands-bethel-a8754416.html.

while awaiting resolution of their cases are under the domain of the state, and even church movements like the sanctuary movement cannot hope to resolve the situation of the millions of refugees denied realistic opportunities for resettlement and/or asylum. Though the risks of politics as statecraft are clear, a more applicable ethical principle in this context would be that of subsidiarity, which teaches that issues must be addressed at the lowest possible institutional level. In this case, for many of the issues discussed in this book, the lowest possible institutional level is the nation-state.

A more complicated question concerns whether the governments of pluralistic nations like the United States or the EU member states are obligated to pursue solidarity with refugees for the reasons outlined in this work. While a full theology of the relation between Christian ethics and the pluralist state exceeds the scope of my argument, I will conclude this question with several brief responses. While I hope that Christians are convinced for Christian reasons to pursue solidarity with refugees, many of the basic policy recommendations that require the state's intervention, such as ensuring due process and avoiding foreign policies that create refugee crises, are policies that would be defensible under a broad commitment to human rights, such as that embodied in the documents of the United Nations, which originated within a pluralistic context and continue to have support in that context today. Christians may interpret the shared discourse of human rights in a variety of ways, treating it as evidence of natural law, common grace, or perhaps as an insufficient ethic in comparison with the entirety of Christian ethics. Yet for present purposes, this common ethic is sufficient to allow for the possibility of reaching majorities who agree with the need to reform the international refugee regime. To those who argue that the biblical commands to care for the migrant are directed toward individuals,[55] it must be added that individual Christians cannot carry out this individual mandate while the state is preventing the migration of refugees. Furthermore, since the militarization of borders is being carried out using tax money, Christians who pay taxes in democratic contexts can rightly express concern when their money is being used in a manner contrary to their conviction. Therefore, conflictual solidarity must extend into the political arena in terms of voting, petitioning, lobbying, protesting, and other political actions.

In Solidarity with Jesus the Refugee

A complete Christian response to the international refugee crisis would extend into a myriad of disciplines and practices, from missiology to social ethics, from the practical institutional design of faith-based nonprofits tasked with aiding in the resettlement of refugees to complex policy packages designed by Christian think tanks and lobbyists intended for promotion in a wide range of political contexts. This exploration of Jesus the Refugee has a far more modest goal, one that is only a part of a full Christian theology and ethic of immigration. I have worked to demonstrate that were the holy family fleeing Herod today, they would not be protected under the international refugee regime. This fact stands as an indictment of the regime itself. The perilous nature of Jesus's refugee status—its fragility in light of the militarization of borders, systemic denial of due process, high standards of the burden of proof, and general

---

55 E.g., Zehnder, *Bible and Immigration*, 254, 258. Zehnder notes that *gēr* is always in the singular, suggesting individual duty and not a duty for the state pertaining to mass (im)migration.

distaste for refugees for (unfounded) national security and economic reasons—illuminates the great need for reform of the current refugee system. The Bible calls us to a general solidarity with strangers, which this chapter has explored in terms of three aspects: incarnational, institutional, and conflictual solidarity. Such solidarity is further clarified by the principles of restitution and relationality, which help identify which refugee groups a given country might prioritize supporting. As such, the circumstances of Jesus the Refugee pose a challenge to the practices of various governments, NGOs, and individual Christians. More than that, in light of the tepid Christian support of refugees in Europe and the United States, the challenge of Jesus the Refugee is a call to repentance for many Christians that they might show solidarity with Jesus the Refugee by seeing modern refugees as Jesus and acting accordingly.

Bibliography

Abrajano, Marisa, and Zoltan L. Hajnal. *White Backlash: Immigration, Race, and American Politics*. Princeton, NJ: Princeton University Press, 2015.

Agier, Michel. *On the Margins of the World: The Refugee Experience Today*. Translated by David Fernbach. Cambridge: Polity, 2008.

Ahn, Ilsup. *Religious Ethics and Migration: Doing Justice to Undocumented Workers*. New York: Routledge, 2014.

Amstutz, Mark R. *Just Immigration: American Policy in Christian Perspective*. Grand Rapids, MI: Eerdmans, 2017.

Amuendo-Dorantes, Catalina, and Susan Pozo. "On the Intended and Unintended Consequences of Enhanced U.S. Border and Interior Immigration Enforcement: Evidence from Mexican Deportees." *Demography* 51, no. 6 (December 2014): 2255–2279.

Ankarlo, Darrell. *Another Man's Sombrero: A Conservative Broadcaster's Undercover Journey across the Mexican Border*. Nashville: Thomas Nelson, 2008.

Aquinas, Thomas. *Summa Theologica*. Translated by Fathers of the Dominican Province. Allen, TX: Christian Classics, 1948.

Bagnall, Roger S. "Army and Police in Roman Upper Egypt." *Journal of the American Research Center in Egypt* 14 (1977): 67–86.

Baker, Scott R. "Effects of Immigrant Legalization on Crime." *American Economic Review* 105, no. 5 (May 2015): 210–213.

Barry, Tom. *Border Wars*. Cambridge, MA: MIT Press, 2011.

Battjes, Hemme. "A Balance between Fairness and Efficiency? The Directive on International Protection and the Dublin Regulation." *European Journal of Migration and Law* 4, no. 2 (April 2002): 159–192.

Bauman, Stephan, Matthew Soerens, and Issam Smeir. *Seeking Refuge: On the Shores of the Global Refugee Crisis*. Chicago: Moody, 2016.

Bavinck, Herman. "Common Grace." Translated by Raymond C. Van Leeuwen. *Calvin Theological Journal* 24, no. 1 (April 1989): 35–65.

Bell, Brian, Francesco Fasani, and Stephen Machin. "Crime and Immigration: Evidence from Large Immigrant Waves." *Review of Economics and Statistics* 95, no. 4 (October 2013): 1278–1290.

Bell, Daniel M., Jr. *Just War as Christian Discipleship: Recentering the Tradition in the Church Rather Than the State*. Grand Rapids, MI: Brazos, 2009.

———. *Liberation Theology after the End of History: The Refusal to Cease Suffering*. New York: Routledge, 2001.

Bellegarde-Smith, Patrick. "Dynastic Dictatorship: The Duvalier Years, 1957–1986." In *Haitian History: New Perspectives*, edited by Alyssa Goldstein Sepinwall, 273–284. New York: Taylor & Francis, 2013.

Ben Zeev, Miriam Pucci. "Jews among Greeks and Romans." In *Early Judaism: A Comprehensive Overview*, edited by John J. Collins and Daniel C. Harlow, 325–342. Grand Rapids, MI: Eerdmans, 2012.

Betts, Alexander, and Paul Collier. *Refuge: Rethinking Refugee Policy in a Changing World*. Oxford: Oxford University Press, 2017.

Bezmozgis, David. "Common Story." In *The Displaced: Refugee Writers on Refugee Lives*, edited by Viet Thanh Nguyen, 43–50. New York: Abrams, 2018.

Biggar, Nigel. "The Value of Limited Loyalty: Christianity, the Nation, and Territorial Boundaries." In *Christian Political Ethics*, edited by James A. Coleman, 92–111. Princeton, NJ: Princeton University Press, 2008.

Bond, Helen K. *The Historical Jesus: A Guide for the Perplexed*. London: Bloomsbury, 2012.

Boot, Max. *The Savage Wars of Peace: Small Wars and the Rise of American Power*. New York: Basic Books, 2002.

Borg, Marcus, and John Dominic Crossan. *The First Christmas: What the Gospels Really Teach about Jesus's Birth*. New York: HarperOne, 1989.

Borjas, George J. *Immigration Economics*. Cambridge, MA: Harvard University Press, 2014.

Bratsberg, Bernt, Oddbjørn Raaum, Marianne Røed, and Pål Schøne. "Immigration Wage Effects by Origin." *Scandinavian Journal of Economics* 116, no. 2 (April 2014): 356–393.

Bretherton, Luke. *Christ and the Common Life: Political Theology and the Case for Democracy*. Grand Rapids, MI: Eerdmans, 2019.

Briggs, Vernon M., Jr. *Mass Immigration and the National Interest*. Armonk, NY: M. E. Sharpe, 1992.

Butcher, Kristin F., Anne Morrison Piehl, and Jay Liao. *Crime, Corrections, and California: What Does Immigration Have to Do with It?* California Counts: Population Trends and Profiles, vol. 9, no. 3 (February 2008).

Butner, D. Glenn, Jr. "Undocumented Prudent Immigrants: De-centering Romans 13 and Rule of Law in Immigration Ethics." *Studies in Christian Ethics* 36, no. 1 (forthcoming).

Callamard, Agnés. "Refugee Women: A Gendered and Political Analysis of the Refugee Experience." In *Refugees: Perspectives on the Experience of Forced Migration*, edited by Alastair Ager, 196–214. London: Pinter, 1999.

Canefe, Nergis. "The Fragmented Nature of the International Refugee Regime and Its Consequences: A Comparative Analysis of the Applications of the 1951 Convention." In *Critical Issues in International Refugee*

Law: Strategies toward Interpretive Harmony, edited by James C. Simeon, 174–210. Cambridge: Cambridge University Press, 2010.

Carroll R., M. Daniel. *The Bible and Borders: Hearing God's Word on Immigration*. Grand Rapids, MI: Brazos, 2020.

Castañeda, Ernesto, and Casey Chiappetta. "Border Residents' Perceptions of Crime and Security in El Paso, Texas." *Social Sciences* 9, no. 3 (2020): 24–39.

Chacón, Jennifer M. "Overcriminalizing Immigration." *Journal of Criminal Law and Criminology* 102, no. 3 (Summer 2012): 615–632.

Chetail, Vincent. "The Common European Asylum System: *Bric-à-brac* or System?" In *Reforming the Common European Asylum System: The New European Refugee Law*, edited by Vincent Chetail, Philippe De Bruycker, and Francesco Maiani, 3–38. Leiden: Brill, 2016.

Clark, Rebecca L., Jeffrey S. Passel, Wendy N. Zimmermann, Michael E. Fix, Taynia L. Mann, and Rosalind E. Berkowitz. *Fiscal Impacts of Undocumented Aliens: Selected Estimates for Seven States*. Washington, DC: Urban Institute, 1994.

Clemens, Michael A., Ethan G. Lewis, and Hannah M. Postel. "Immigration Restrictions as Active Labor Market Policy: Evidence from the Mexican Bracero Exclusion." *American Economic Review* 108, no. 6 (June 2018): 1468–1487.

Clune, Michael S. "The Fiscal Impacts of Immigrants: A California Case Study." In *The Immigration Debate: Studies on the Economic, Demographic, and Fiscal Effects of Immigration*, edited by James P. Smith and Barry Edmonston, 120–182. Washington, DC: National Academy Press, 1998.

Cohen, Shaye J. D. *From the Maccabees to the Mishnah*. 2nd ed. Louisville, KY: Westminster John Knox, 2006.

Colwell, Matthew. "Proclaiming Liberty to the Captives: Amalia Molina." In *Our God Is Undocumented: Biblical Faith and Immigrant Justice*, edited by Ched Myers and Matthew Colwell, 107–122. Maryknoll, NY: Orbis, 2012.

Cooray, Arusha, and Friedrich Schneider. "Does Corruption Promote Emigration? An Empirical Examination." *Journal of Population Economics* 29, no. 1 (January 2016): 293–310.

Cope, Lamar. "Matthew XXV:31–46: 'The Sheep and the Goats' Reinterpreted." *Novum Testamentum* 11, nos. 1/2 (January–April 1969): 32–44.

Cortes, Kalena E. "Are Refugees Different from Economic Immigrants? Some Empirical Evidence on the Heterogeneity of Immigrant Groups in the United States." *Review of Economics and Statistics* 86, no. 2 (May 2004): 465–480.

Cosgrove, Charles. *Appealing to Scripture in Moral Debate: Five Hermeneutical Rules*. Grand Rapids, MI: Eerdmans, 2002.

Crawley, Heaven, and Katharine Jones. "Beyond Here and There: (Re)conceptualizing Migrant Journeys and the 'In-Between.'" *Journal of Ethnic and Migration Studies* 47, no. 14 (2021): 3226–3242.

Crone, Manni, Maja Felicia Falkentoft, and Teemu Tammikko. *Europe's Refugee Crisis and the Threat of Terrorism: An Extraordinary Threat?* Danish Institute for International Studies Report. Copenhagen, Denmark: January 1, 2017.

Dakin-Grimm, Linda. *Dignity and Justice: Welcoming the Stranger at Our Border*. Maryknoll, NY: Orbis, 2020.

Decker, Christopher, Jerry Deichert, and Lourdes Gouveia. *Nebraska's Immigrant Population: Economic and Fiscal Impacts*. OLLAS Special Report No. 5. Omaha, NE: Office of Latino/Latin American Studies (OLLAS), University of Nebraska at Omaha, 2008.

De La Torre, Miguel A. *Trails of Hope and Terror: Testimonies on Immigration*. Maryknoll, NY: Orbis, 2009.

———. *The U.S. Immigration Crisis: Toward an Ethics of Place*. Eugene, OR: Cascade, 2016.

Dinçir, Osman Bahadir, et al. *Turkey and Syrian Refugees: The Limits of Hospitality*. Washington, DC: Brookings Institute, 2013.

Donnelly, Ellen A., and John M. MacDonald. "The Downstream Effects of Bail and Pretrial Detention on Racial Disparities in Incarceration." *Journal of Criminal Law and Criminology* 108, no. 4 (2018): 775–814.

Drollinger, Ralph. *What the Bible Says about Our Illegal Immigration Problem*. Phoenix, AZ: Capital Ministries, 2016.

Duke, Karen, Rosemary Sales, and Jeanne Gregory. "Refugee Resettlement in Europe." In *Refugees, Citizenship, and Social Policy in Europe*, edited by Alice Bloch and Carl Levy, 105–131. London: Macmillan, 1999.

Eichstaedt, Peter. *Dangerous Divide: Peril and Promise on the US-Mexico Border*. Chicago: Lawrence Hill, 2014.

Espenshade, Thomas, and Gregory Huber. "Fiscal Impacts of Immigrants and the Shrinking Welfare State." In *The Handbook of International Migration: The American Experience*, edited by Charles Hirschman, Philip Kasinitz, and Josh Dewind, 360–370. New York: Russell Sage, 1999.

Faist, Thomas, Margit Fauser, and Eveline Reisenauer. *Transnational Migration*. Malden, MA: Polity, 2013.

Ferraro, Vincent A. *Immigrants and Crime in the New Destinations*. El Paso: LFB Scholarly, 2014.

Fiddian-Qasmiyeh, Elena. "Gender and Forced Migration." In *The Oxford Handbook of Refugee and Forced Migration Studies*, edited by Elena Fiddian-Qasmiyeh, Gil Loescher, Katy Long, and Nando Sigona, 395–408. Oxford: Oxford University Press, 2014.

Fitzgerald, David Scott. *Refuge beyond Reach: How Rich Democracies Repel Asylum Seekers*. Oxford: Oxford University Press, 2019.

Foged, Mette, and Giovanni Peri. "Immigrants' Effect on Native Workers: New Analysis on Longitudinal Data." *American Economic Journal: Applied Economics* 8, no. 2 (2016): 1–34.

Foreman, Benjamin A. "Matthew's Birth Narrative: Matt 2:1–18." In *Lexham Geographic Commentary on the Gospels*, edited by Barry J. Beitzel and Kristopher A. Lyle, 19–21. Bellingham, WA: Lexington, 2017.

Forrester, Andrew, and Alex Nowrasteh. *Do Immigration Enforcement Programs Reduce Crime? Evidence from the 287(g) Program in North Carolina*. Washington, DC: Cato Institute, 2018.

France, R. T. *The Gospel of Matthew*. Grand Rapids, MI: Eerdmans, 2007.

Fredriksen, Paula. *From Jesus to Christ: The Origins of the New Testament Image of Jesus*. New Haven, CT: Yale University Press, 2000.

Gambetti, Sandra. *The Alexandrian Riots of 38 C.E. and the Persecution of the Jews: A Historical Reconstruction*. Leiden: Brill, 2009.

Gammeltoft-Hansen, Thomas. *Access to Asylum: International Refugee Law and the Globalisation of Migration Control*. Cambridge: Cambridge University Press, 2011.

García, María Christina. *The Refugee Challenge in Post–Cold War America*. Oxford: Oxford University Press, 2017.

———. *Seeking Refuge: Central American Migration to Mexico, the United States, and Canada*. Berkeley: University of California Press, 2006.

Gatrell, Peter. *The Making of the Modern Refugee*. Oxford: Oxford University Press, 2013.

Ghosh, Jayati. "Fear of Foreigners: Recession and Racism in Europe." *Race/Ethnicity: Multidisciplinary Global Contexts* 4, no. 2 (Winter 2011): 183–190.

Gilliard, Dominique DuBois. *Rethinking Incarceration: Advocating for Justice That Restores*. Downers Grove, IL: InterVarsity Academic, 2018.

Glanville, Mark R., and Luke Glanville. *Refuge Reimagined: Biblical Kinship in Global Politics*. Downers Grove, IL: InterVarsity Academic, 2021.

Goodwin-Gill, Guy S. "The International Law of Refugee Protection." In *The Oxford Handbook of Refugee and Forced Migration Studies*, edited by Elena Fiddian-Qasmiyeh, Gil Loescher, Katy Long, and Nando Sigona, 36–47. Oxford: Oxford University Press, 2014.

Goodwin-Gill, Guy S., and Jane McAdam. *The Refugee in International Law*. 3rd ed. Oxford: Oxford University Press, 2007.

Goss, Stephen, Alice Wade, J. Patrick Skirvin, Michael Morris, K. Mark Bye, and Danielle Huston. *Effects of Unauthorized Immigration on the Actuarial Status of the Social Security Trust Funds.* Actuarial Note 151. Baltimore, MD: Social Security Administration Office of the Chief Actuary, 2013.

Gregory, Andy. "Family Shielded from Deportation in Dutch Church for Three Months Finally Granted Asylum." *Independent,* January 31, 2019. https://www.independent.co.uk/news/world/dutch-church-family -deportation-granted-asylum-tamrazyan-netherlands-bethel-a8754416 .html.

Grosby, Steven. "Borders, Territory and Nationality in the Ancient Near East and Armenia." *Journal of the Economic and Social History of the Orient* 40, no. 1 (1997): 1–29.

Grouev, Ivaylo, ed. *Bullets on the Water: Refugee Stories.* London: McGill-Queen's University Press, 2000.

Gruen, Eric S. "Judaism in the Diaspora." In *Early Judaism: A Comprehensive Overview,* edited by John J. Collins and Daniel C. Harlow, 113–132. Grand Rapids, MI: Eerdmans, 2012.

Haddad, Emma. *The Refugee in International Society: Between Sovereigns.* Cambridge: Cambridge University Press, 2008.

Hagan, John, and Alberto Palloni. "Immigration and Crime in the United States." In *The Immigration Debate: Studies on the Economic, Demographic, and Fiscal Effects of Immigration,* edited by James P. Smith and Barry Edmonston, 367–387. Washington, DC: National Academy Press, 1998.

Haines, David W. *Immigration Structures and Immigrant Lives: An Introduction to the US Experience.* Lanham, MD: Rowman & Littlefield, 2017.

Halsall, Guy. *Barbarian Migrations and the Roman West 376–568.* Cambridge: Cambridge University Press, 2007.

Hamilton, Mark W. *Jesus, King of Strangers: What the Bible Really Says about Immigration.* Grand Rapids, MI: Eerdmans, 2019.

Hamlin, Rebecca. "Ideology, International Law, and the INS: The Development of American Asylum Politics 1948–Present." *Polity* 47, no. 3 (July 2015): 320–336.

Hawkins, J. Russell. *The Bible Told Them So: How Southern Evangelicals Fought to Preserve White Supremacy.* Oxford: Oxford University Press, 2021.

Hawthorn, Robert. "The Fiscal Impact of Immigration on the Advanced Economies." *Oxford Review of Economic Policy* 24, no. 3 (Autumn 2008): 560–580.

Hays, Richard B. *The Moral Vision of the New Testament: A Contemporary Introduction to New Testament Ethics.* New York: Harper Collins, 1996.

Heater, Derek. *A Brief History of Citizenship.* Edinburgh: Edinburgh University Press, 2004.

Herlihy, Jane, Laura Jobson, and Stuart Turner. "Just Tell Us What Happened to You: Autobiographical Memory and Seeking Asylum." *Applied Cognitive Psychology* 26, no. 5 (September/October 2012): 661–676.

Herman, Geoffrey. "The Jews of Parthian Babylonia." In *The Parthian Empire and Its Religions: Studies in the Dynamics of Religious Diversity*, edited by Peter Wick and Markus Zehnder, 141–150. Gutenberg, Germany: Computus Druck Satz and Verlag, 2012.

Heyer, Kristin E. *Kinship across Borders: A Christian Ethic of Immigration.* Washington, DC: Georgetown University Press, 2012.

Hiers, Richard H. *Justice and Compassion in Biblical Law.* New York: Continuum, 2009.

Hoffmeier, James K. *The Immigration Crisis: Immigrants, Aliens, and the Bible.* Wheaton, IL: Crossway, 2009.

Hourwich, I. A. "Immigration and Crime." *American Journal of Sociology* 17, no. 4 (January 1912): 478–490.

Houston, Fleur S. *You Shall Love the Stranger as Yourself: The Bible, Refugees, and Asylum.* London: Routledge, 2015.

Hunter, James Davison. *To Change the World: The Irony, Tragedy, and Possibility of Christianity in the Late Modern World.* Oxford: Oxford University Press, 2010.

Increasing Costs of Illegal Immigration: Hearing before the Committee on Appropriations, United States Senate, One Hundred Third Congress, Section Session, Special Hearing. Washington, DC: US GPO, 1994.

Ishay, Micheline R. *The History of Human Rights: From Ancient Times to the Globalization Era.* Berkeley: University of California Press, 2008.

Jacklin, Jillian Marie. "The Cuban Criminal: Media Reporting and the Production of a Popular Image." *International Journal of Cuban Studies* 11, no. 1 (Summer 2019): 61–83.

Jones, Reece. *Violent Borders: Refugees and the Right to Move.* London: Verso, 2016.

Josephus. *The Antiquities of the Jews.* Translated by William Whiston. New York: Lovell & Coryell, n.d., ca. 1900s.

Kaemingk, Matthew. *Christian Hospitality and Muslim Immigration in an Age of Fear.* Grand Rapids, MI: Eerdmans, 2018.

Kälin, Walter. "Internal Displacement." In *The Oxford Handbook of Refugee and Forced Migration Studies*, edited by Elena Fiddian-Qasmiyeh, Gil Loescher, Katy Long, and Nando Sigona, 163–175. Oxford: Oxford University Press, 2014.

Kasarda, John D., and James H. Johnson Jr. *The Economic Impact of the Hispanic Population on the State of North Carolina.* Chapel Hill, NC: Frank Hawkins Kenan Institute of Private Enterprise, 2006.

Keener, Craig S. *A Commentary on the Gospel of Matthew.* Grand Rapids, MI: Eerdmans, 1999.

Kelly, Rebecca, Thomas J. Doherty, Thomas Gabel, and Willa Disbrow. "Large Carnivore Attacks on Humans: The State of Knowledge." *Human Ecology Review* 25, no. 2 (2019): 15–34.

Kendall, Wesley. *From Gulag to Guantanamo: Political, Social and Economic Evolutions of Mass Incarceration.* London: Rowman & Littlefield, 2016.

Kim, Matthew D. *Preaching with Cultural Intelligence: Understanding the People Who Hear Our Sermons.* Grand Rapids, MI: Baker Academic, 2017.

Kitani, Kanan. "Jesus the Paradigmatic Migrant." In *Christian Theology in the Age of Migration: Implications for World Christianity*, edited by Peter C. Phan, 129–150. Lanham, MD: Lexington, 2020.

Kneebone, Susan. *Refugees, Asylum Seekers and the Rule of Law: Comparative Perspectives*. Cambridge: Cambridge University Press, 2009.

Konczal, Lisa, and Alex Stepik. "Haiti." In *The New Americans: A Guide to Immigration since 1965*, edited by Mary C. Waters, Reed Ueda, and Helen B. Marrow, 445–457. Cambridge, MA: Harvard University Press, 2007.

Laird, Lorelei. "Legal Logjam: Neglect and Political Interference Have Created a Growing Backlog in Immigration Courts of 540,000-plus Cases." *ABA Journal* 103, no. 4 (April 2017): 52–59.

Lee, Matthew T., Ramiro Martinez Jr., and Richard Rosenfeld. "Does Immigration Increase Homicide? Negative Evidence from Three Border Cities." *Sociological Quarterly* 42, no. 4 (Autumn 2001): 559–580.

Lee, Ronald D., and Timothy W. Miller. "The Current Fiscal Impact of Immigrants and Their Descendants: Beyond the Immigrant Household." In *The Immigration Debate: Studies on the Economic, Demographic, and Fiscal Effects of Immigration*, edited by James P. Smith and Barry Edmonston, 183–205. Washington, DC: National Academy Press, 1998.

Lehmann, Paul. "Haitian Refugees." In *Immigrants, Refugees, and U.S. Policy*, edited by Grant S. McClellan, 87–92. New York: H. W. Wilson, 1981.

Lennox, Malissia. "Refugees, Racism, and Reparations: A Critique of the United States' Haitian Immigration Policy." *Stanford Law Review* 45, no. 3 (February 1993): 687–724.

Léonard, Sarah, and Christian Kaunert. *Refugees, Security, and the European Union*. London: Routledge, 2019.

Levy, Ian Christopher. *Introducing Medieval Biblical Interpretation: The Senses of Scripture in Premodern Exegesis*. Grand Rapids, MI: Baker, 2018.

Loescher, Gil, and Ann Dull Loescher. *The Global Refugee Crisis: A Reference Handbook*. Santa Barbara, CA: ABC-CLIO, 1994.

Long, Clara, et al. *They Treat You like You Are Worthless: Internal DHS Reports of Abuse by US Border Officials.* New York: Human Rights Watch, 2021. Accessed October 22, 2021. https://www.hrw.org/sites/default/files/media_2021/10/us_borderabuses1021_web.pdf.

Loyd, Jenna M., and Alison Mountz. *Boats, Borders, and Bases: Race, the Cold War, and the Rise of Migration Detention in the United States.* Oakland: University of California Press, 2018.

Luther, Martin. "The Day of the Holy Innocents." In *The Complete Sermons of Martin Luther,* vol. 7, edited by Eugene F. A. Klug, translated by Eugene F. A. Klug, Erwin W. Koehlinger, James Lanning, Everette W. Meier, Dorothy Schocnecht, and Allen Schuldheiss, 255–264. Grand Rapids, MI: Baker, 2000.

Lydgate, Joanna. *Assembly-Line Justice: A Review of Operation Streamline.* Berkeley, CA: Chief Justice Earl Warren Institute on Race, Ethnicity & Diversity, 2010. https://www.law.berkeley.edu/files/Operation_Streamline_Policy_Brief.pdf.

MacDonald, John M., John R. Hipp, and Charlotte Gill. "The Effects of Immigrant Concentration on Changes in Neighborhood Crime Rates." *Journal of Quantitative Criminology* 29, no. 2 (June 2013): 191–215.

Martens, Peter L. "Immigrants, Crime, and Criminal Justice in Sweden." *Crime and Justice* 21 (1997): 183–255.

Martinez, Ramiro, Jr., and Matthew T. Lee. "Comparing the Context of Immigrant Homicides in Miami: Haitians, Jamaicans, and Mariels." *International Migration Review* 34, no. 3 (Autumn 2000): 794–812.

Massey, Douglas S., Joaquin Arango, Grame Hugo, Ali Kouaouci, Adela Pellegrino, and J. Edward Taylor. "An Evaluation of International Migration Theory: The North American Case." *Population and Development Review* 20, no. 4 (December 1994): 699–751.

Mastrobuoni, Giovanni, and Paolo Pinotti. "Legal Status and the Criminal Activity of Immigrants." *American Economic Journal: Applied Economics* 7, no. 2 (April 2015): 175–206.

Matthews, Victor H. *A Brief History of Ancient Israel.* Louisville, KY: Westminster John Knox, 2002.

Maystadt, Jean-François, and Philip Verwimp. "Winners and Losers among a Refugee-Hosting Population." *Economic Development and Cultural Change* 62, no. 4 (July 2014): 769–809.

McCaulley, Esau. *Reading While Black: African American Biblical Interpretation as an Exercise in Hope.* Downers Grove, IL: InterVarsity Academic, 2020.

McGuire, Daniel C. "Cooperation with Evil." In *The Westminster Dictionary of Christian Ethics*, edited by James F. Childress and John Macquarrie, 129. Philadelphia: Westminster John Knox, 1986.

McLaughlin, Raoul. *The Roman Empire and the Silk Routes: The Ancient World Economy and the Empires of Parthia, Central Asia, and Han China.* Barnsley, UK: Pen & Sword, 2016.

Miles, Thomas J., and Adam B. Cox. "Does Immigration Enforcement Reduce Crime? Evidence from Secure Communities." *Journal of Law & Economics* 57, no. 4 (November 2014): 937–973.

Miller, David. *Strangers in Our Midst: The Political Philosophy of Immigration.* Cambridge: Harvard University Press, 2016.

Milton, Daniel, Megan Spencer, and Michael Findley. "Radicalism of the Hopeless: Refugee Flows and Transnational Terrorism." *International Interactions: Empirical and Theoretical Research in International Relations* 39, no. 5 (2013): 621–645.

Monyak, Suzanne. "Garland Withdraws Asylum Limits for Domestic Abuse Victims." *Roll Call*, June 16, 2021. https://rollcall.com/2021/06/16/garland-withdraws-asylum-limits-for-domestic-abuse-victims/.

Morris, Ellen. "Prevention through Deterrence along Egypt's Northeastern Border: Or the Politics of a Weaponized Desert." *Journal of Eastern Mediterranean Archaeology & Heritage Studies* 5, no. 2 (2017): 133–147.

Mott, Stephen Charles. *Biblical Ethics and Social Change.* Oxford: Oxford University Press, 1982.

Musolf, Gil Richard. "The Asylum-Seeking Process: An American Tradition." In *Conflict and Forced Migration: Escape from Oppression and Stories of Survival, Resilience, and Hope*, edited by Gil Richard Musolf, 11–42. Bingley, UK: Emerald, 2019.

Nathwani, Niraj. *Rethinking Refugee Law: Refugees and Human Rights*. New York: Martinus Nijhoff, 2003.

Neusner, Jacob. *A History of the Jews in Babylonia. I—The Parthian Period*. Leiden: Brill, 1969.

Ngewa, Samuel M. "Pneumatology: Its Implications for the African Context." In *The Spirit over the Earth: Pneumatology in the Majority World*, edited by Gene L. Green, Stephen T. Pardue, and K. K. Yeo, 99–121. Grand Rapids, MI: Eerdmans, 2016.

"NGO Statement on Voluntary Repatriation (22–24 May 2002)." *Refugee Survey Quarterly* 22, nos. 2/3 (2003): 420–428.

Nicols, John. *Civic Patronage in the Roman Empire*. Leiden: Brill, 2013.

Noll, Gregor. "Article 31." In *The 1951 Convention Relating to the Status of Refugees and Its 1967 Protocol: A Commentary*, edited by Andreas Zimmermann, Jonas Dörschner, and Felix Machts, 1243–1276. Oxford: Oxford University Press, 2011.

Nolland, John. *The Gospel of Matthew*. Grand Rapids, MI: Eerdmans, 2005.

North, David, and Marion Houstoun. *The Characteristics and Role of Illegal Aliens in the U.S. Labor Market: An Exploratory Study*. Washington, DC: Linton, 1976.

Nowrasteh, Alex. *Terrorists by Immigration Status and Nationality: A Risk Analysis, 1975–2017*. Washington, DC: Cato Institute, 2019.

Nullens, Patrick, and Ronald T. Michener. *The Matrix of Christian Ethics: Integrating Philosophy and Moral Theology in a Postmodern Context*. Colorado Springs: Paternoster, 2010.

Nunziata, Luca. "Immigration and Crime: Evidence from Victimization Data." *Journal of Population Economics* 28, no. 3 (July 2015): 697–736.

Oliver, Kelly. "Abolish Refugee Detention." In *Refugees Now: Rethinking Borders, Hospitality, and Citizenship*, edited by Kelly Oliver, Lisa M. Madura, and Sabeen Ahmed, 117–136. London: Rowman & Littlefield, 2019.

Owen, David. "Refugees and the Politics of Indignity." In *Refugees Now: Rethinking Borders, Hospitality, and Citizenship*, edited by Kelly Oliver, Lisa M. Madura, and Sabeen Ahmed, 13–26. London: Rowman & Littlefield, 2019.

———. *What Do We Owe to Refugees?* Medford, MA: Polity, 2020.

Pacheco, Gilda. *Nicaraguan Refugees in Costa Rica: Adjustment to Camp Life.* Washington, DC: Center for Immigration Policy and Refugee Assistance, 1989.

Parekh, Serena. *No Refuge: Ethics and the Global Refugee Crisis.* Oxford: Oxford University Press, 2020.

Parker, Richard A., and Louis M. Rea. *Illegal Immigration in San Diego County: An Analysis of Costs and Revenues.* San Diego, CA: Rea & Parker, 1993.

Pew Research. "Liberal Democrats Most Likely to Favor Admitting Refugees from Afghanistan." September 23, 2021. https://www.pewresearch.org/politics/2021/09/23/biden-administrations-handling-of-afghanistan-and-views-of-accepting-afghan-refugees-in-the-u-s/pp_2021-09-23_biden-approval_03-02/.

Pico, Juan Hernández. "Solidarity with the Poor and the Unity of the Church." In *Theology of Christian Solidarity*, translated by Phillip Berryman, 43–98. Maryknoll, NY: Orbis, 1985.

Piehl, Anne Morrison. "Testimony of Anne Morrison Piehl, Ph.D., Department of Economics and Program in Criminal Justice, Rutgers, the State University of New Jersey." In *Comprehensive Immigration Reform: Impact of Immigration on States and Localities. Hearing before the Subcommittee on Immigration, Citizenship, Refugees, Border Security, and International Law of the Committee on the Judiciary, House of*

Representatives, One Hundred Tenth Congress, 81–90. Washington, DC: US GPO, 2007.

Pinsker, Matt C. *Crisis on the Border: An Eyewitness Account of Illegal Aliens, Violent Crime, and Cartels*. Washington, DC: Regnery, 2020.

Pius XII. *Exsul Familia Nazarethana* (1952). Papal Encyclicals Online. Accessed December 12, 2021. https://www.papalencyclicals.net/pius12/p12exsul.htm.

Quezada, Sarah. *Love Undocumented: Risking Trust in a Fearful World*. Harrisonburg, VA: Herald, 2018.

Rajendra, Tisha M. *Migrants and Citizens: Justice and Responsibility in the Ethics of Immigration*. Grand Rapids, MI: Eerdmans, 2017.

Regan, Margaret. *The Death of Josseline: Immigration Stories from the Arizona-Mexico Borderlands*. Boston: Beacon, 2010.

Rodd, Cyril S. *Glimpses of a Strange Land: Studies in Old Testament Ethics*. Edinburgh: T&T Clark, 2001.

Sampaio, Anna. *Terrorizing Latina/o Immigrants: Race, Gender, and Immigration Politics in the Age of Security*. Philadelphia: Temple University Press, 2015.

Sánchez, George J. "Face the Nation: Race, Immigration, and the Rise of Nativism in Late-Twentieth Century America." In *The Handbook of International Migration: The American Experience*, edited by Charles Hirschman, Philip Kasinitz, and Josh Dewind, 371–382. New York: Russell Sage, 1999.

Sanders, E. P. *The Historical Figure of Jesus*. London: Penguin, 1993.

Santa Ana, Otto. *Brown Tide Rising: Metaphors of Latinos in Contemporary American Public Discourse*. Austin: University of Texas Press, 2002.

Sassen, Saskia. *The Mobility of Labor and Capital: A Study in the International Investment and Labor Flow*. Cambridge: Cambridge University Press, 1988.

Schäfer, Peter. *Judeophobia: Attitudes toward the Jews in the Ancient World*. Cambridge, MA: Harvard University Press, 1997.

Schiller, Nina Glick, and Thomas Faist, eds. *Migration, Development, and Transnationalization: A Critical Stance*. New York: Berghahn, 2010.

Schlude, Jason M., and J. Andrew Overman. "Herod the Great: A Near Eastern Case Study in Roman-Parthian Politics." In *Arsacids, Romans and Local Elites: Cross-Cultural Interactions of the Parthian Empire*, edited by Jason Schlude and Benjamin Rubin, 93–110. Oxford: Oxbow, 2017.

Slack, Jeremy, Daniel Martínez, Scott Whiteford, and Emily Peiffer. "In Harm's Way: Family Separation, Immigration Enforcement Programs, and Security on the U.S.-Mexico Border." In *The Shadow of the Wall: Violence and Migration on the U.S.-Mexico Border*, edited by Jeremy Slack, Daniel E. Martínez, and Scott Whiteford, 73–93. Tucson: University of Arizona Press, 2018.

Slack, Jeremy, and Scott Whiteford. "Violence and Migration on the Arizona-Sonora Border." In *The Shadow of the Wall: Violence and Migration on the U.S.-Mexico Border*, edited by Jeremy Slack, Daniel E. Martínez, and Scott Whiteford, 43–62. Tucson: University of Arizona Press, 2018.

Sobrino, Jon. "Bearing with One Another in Faith." In *Theology of Christian Solidarity*, translated by Phillip Berryman, 1–42. Maryknoll, NY: Orbis, 1985.

Soerens, Matthew, and Jenny Yang. *Welcoming the Stranger: Justice, Compassion, and Truth in the Immigration Debate*. Rev. ed. Downers Grove, IL: InterVarsity Books, 2018.

Song, Choan-Seng. *Third-Eye Theology: Theology in Formation in Asian Settings*. Maryknoll, NY: Orbis, 1979.

Spagat, Elliot. "US Identifies 3,900 Children Separated at Border under Trump." *Associated Press News*, June 8, 2021. https://apnews.com/article/az-state-wire-donald-trump-immigration-lifestyle-government-and-politics-54e2e5bbff270019d8bda3c81161c7c7.

Staffans, Ida. *Evidence in European Asylum Procedures*. Leiden: Martinus Nijhoff, 2012.

Stansfield, Richard, Scott Akins, Rubén G. Rumbaut, and Roger B. Hammer. "Assessing the Effects of Recent Immigration on Serious Property Crime in Austin, Texas." *Sociological Perspectives* 56, no. 4 (Winter 2013): 647–672.

Stern, Lewis M. "Response to Vietnamese Refugees: Surveys of Public Opinion." *Social Work* 26, no. 4 (July 1981): 306–311.

Strayhorn, Carole Keeton. *Undocumented Immigrants in Texas: A Financial Analysis of the Impact to the State Budget and Economy.* Office of the Comptroller. Austin, TX: December 2006.

Sullivan, Eileen. "U.S. Accelerated Expulsion of Haitian Migrants in May." *New York Times*, June 9, 2022. https://www.nytimes.com/2022/06/09/us/politics/haiti-migrants-biden.html.

Swinton, John. *Raging with Compassion: Pastoral Responses to the Problem of Evil.* Grand Rapids, MI: Eerdmans, 2007.

Thielman, Frank. *Theology of the New Testament: A Canonical and Synthetic Approach.* Grand Rapids, MI: Zondervan, 2005.

Thompson, Charles D., Jr. *Border Odyssey: Travels along the U.S./Mexico Divide.* Austin: University of Texas Press, 2015.

Turner, William Clair, Jr. *Preaching That Makes the Word Plain: Doing Theology in the Crucible of Life.* Eugene, OR: Cascade, 2008.

Uganda Bureau of Statistics. *Uganda National Household Survey 2016/2017 Report.* Kampala, Uganda: Uganda Bureau of Statistics, 2017. Accessed October 25, 2021. https://www.ubos.org/wp-content/uploads/publications/03_20182016_UNHS_FINAL_REPORT.pdf.

Van Houten, Christiana. *The Alien in Israelite Law.* Journal for the Study of the Old Testament Supplement Series 107. Sheffield, UK: JSOT, 1991.

Vella, Danielle. *Dying to Live: Stories from Refugees on the Road to Freedom.* Lanham, MD: Rowman & Littlefield, 2020.

Verdirame, Guglielmo, and Barbara Harrell-Bond. *Rights in Exile: Janus-Faced Humanitarianism.* New York: Berghahn, 2005.

Vermes, Geza. *The Real Jesus: Then and Now*. Minneapolis: Fortress, 2010.

Walczak, Bartłomiej, and Nikolaos Lampas. "Beliefs on Refugees as a Terrorist Threat: The Social Determinants of Refugee-Related Stereotypes." *Studia Migracyjne Przegląd Polonijny* 176, no. 2 (2020): 53–70.

Walker, Kristin. "Defending the 1951 Convention Definition of Refugee." *Georgetown Immigration Law Journal* 17, no. 4 (2003): 583–609.

Walzer, Michael. *Spheres of Justice: A Defense of Pluralism and Equality*. New York: Basic Books, 1983.

Webber, Leanne, and Sharon Pickering. *Globalization and Borders: Death at the Global Frontier*. New York: Palgrave Macmillan, 2011.

Weintraub, Sidney, and Gilberto Cardenas. *The Use of Public Services by Undocumented Aliens in Texas: A Study of State Costs and Revenues*. Policy Research Report, no. 60. Austin, TX: Lyndon B. Johnson School of Public Affairs, 1984.

Wike, Richard, Bruce Stokes, and Katie Simmons. "Europeans Fear Wave of Refugees Will Mean More Terrorism, Fewer Jobs: Sharp Ideological Divides across EU on Views about Minorities, Diversity, and National Identity." Pew Research Center, July 11, 2016. https://www.pewresearch.org/global/2016/07/11/europeans-fear-wave-of-refugees-will-mean-more-terrorism-fewer-jobs/.

Wiley, James. "Undocumented Aliens and Recognized Refugees: The Right to Work in Costa Rica." *International Migration Review* 29, no. 2 (Summer 1995): 423–440.

Wilsher, Daniel. *Immigration Detention: Law, History, and Politics*. Cambridge: Cambridge University Press, 2011.

Witherington, Ben, III. *New Testament History: A Narrative Account*. Grand Rapids, MI: Baker Academic, 2001.

Wood, Susan K. "Catholic Reception of the Joint Declaration on the Doctrine of Justification." In *Rereading Paul Together: Protestant and Catholic Perspectives on Justification*, edited by David E. Aune, 43–59. Grand Rapids, MI: Baker Academic, 2006.

Wright, Christopher J. H. *Old Testament Ethics for the People of God*. Downers Grove, IL: InterVarsity Academic, 2004.

Wright, N. T. *The New Testament and the People of God*. Minneapolis: Fortress, 1992.

Zehnder, Markus. *The Bible and Immigration: A Critical and Empirical Reassessment*. Eugene, OR: Pickwick, 2021.

Zimmermann, Andreas, and Claudia Mahler. "Article 1 A, para. 2." In *The 1951 Convention Relating to the Status of Refugees and Its 1967 Protocol: A Commentary*, edited by Andreas Zimmermann, Jonas Dörschner, and Felix Machts, 281–465. Oxford: Oxford University Press, 2011.

Zolberg, Aristide R. *A Nation by Design: Immigration Policy in the Fashioning of America*. Cambridge, MA: Harvard University Press, 2006.

Index of Names

Subject Index

Scripture Index